THE MOST COMPLETE AND EASY-TO-FOLLOW FLORIDA DMV EXAM HANDBOOK WITH 250 PRACTICE QUESTIONS

Our Comprehensive, Up-To-Date Guide Will Make it Effortless to Pass Your Permit Test

DRIVE SAFELY PUBLISHING

CONTENTS

LEGAL DISCLAIMER

The QR codes for the downloadable flashcards and audio files for the practice exams are located on the last page of the book.

This handbook has been created with the utmost care and dedication to providing accurate, helpful, and comprehensive information regarding the rules, regulations, and procedures associated with driving in the state of Florida.

However, it is crucial to understand that this handbook is intended solely for educational purposes and as a guide to assist individuals in preparing for the Florida Department of Motor Vehicles (DMV) knowledge examination. It does not replace or supersede any official publications or regulations provided by the Florida DMV or any other relevant legal authorities.

The author, instructors, and publishers of this handbook shall not be held responsible or liable for any actions, incidents, accidents, or consequences that may occur as a result of applying the information provided within this book. Driving is an intricate and dynamic activity, and while we strive to offer accurate guidance, we cannot anticipate or control the specific circumstances and decisions made by individual drivers.

Driving comes with great responsibility. It is the driver's sole responsibility to adhere to all applicable laws, regulations, and guidelines provided by the Florida DMV and other relevant authorities. This handbook should be used in conjunction with official DMV resources and instruction from certified driving instructors.

For specific questions, concerns, or legal advice regarding your driving privileges, it is strongly recommended that you consult with qualified legal professionals or officials from the Florida DMV.

Please be aware that laws, regulations, and procedures related to driving can change over time. While we strive to keep this handbook as up-to-date as possible, it is essential for readers to verify information with the latest official sources, such as the Florida DMV's official publications and website. Please <u>DO NOT</u> go directly to the practice exams, it is vital that you read the material in the chapters as the questions presented on the official exam can vary in wording significantly, by reading the material you will be able to better decipher the correct answer for the question.

By using this handbook, you acknowledge and accept the terms of this disclaimer, understanding that you are solely responsible for your actions and decisions while driving in the state of Florida.

Safe and responsible driving is of paramount importance, and we encourage all readers to prioritize safety, respect traffic laws, and continuously improve their knowledge and skills as responsible drivers.

INTRODUCTION

In the golden light of a Florida morning, the road stretches ahead, promising landscapes from sun-soaked coastlines to lush wetlands. But before you can embrace the freedom of the open road, you face a formidable challenge: the Florida DMV exam.

Imagine yourself in a nondescript room, clutching a pamphlet that resembles an encrypted treasure map. Nervous anticipation fills the air as you sit among fellow aspiring drivers, all on the verge of beginning their motoring journeys.

Hours of studying traffic laws and memorizing road signs have brought you to this moment, yet anxiety looms. What if you fail? What if the test proves more complex than expected? Regardless of age, the Florida DMV exam can seem like an insurmountable obstacle.

Now, envision a guide that transforms this daunting task into a manageable endeavor. A handbook that simplifies driving rules, preparing you for success and unlocking the path to freedom, confidence, and Florida sunsets.

As you hold this book, you're on a journey to conquer a challenge. It may be the allure of freedom or a determination to navigate bureaucracy. Or perhaps you're a parent, guiding your child toward driving independence, yearning to equip them with the knowledge and confidence they need.

You see, beyond the title of this book lies a shared understanding—the understanding that this journey is about more than just passing a test. It's about empowerment. It's the thrill of merging onto the freeway for the first time, the gratification of navigating complex intersections flawlessly, and the sense of pride in becoming a responsible, confident driver. This book goes beyond memorizing rules; it provides the tools to navigate life's pathways with confidence. Here's a glimpse of the invaluable insights this book offers:

- **Simplified learning:** The intricacies of driving laws and regulations are meticulously explained within these pages. Written in clear, concise language, you'll swiftly understand fundamental concepts that may have previously seemed puzzling.
- **Effective study guide:** The comprehensive content of the official DMV handbook is skillfully broken down into easily understandable sections, promoting structured learning. It's time to say bye to the specter of information overload; this book's structured approach simplifies your study process, rendering it far more efficient and manageable.
- **Comprehensive practice questions:** Encompassing an expansive array of practice questions, this book pushes you beyond mere memorization. Immerse yourself in exercises that simulate the real DMV test environment, honing your ability to apply learned concepts and familiarizing you with the test format.
- **Real-life driving scenarios:** While the DMV test assesses your theoretical understanding of the law, it's on the road where the knowledge truly comes to life. This book doesn't just prepare you for the test; it equips you for real-world

driving scenarios, bridging the divide between theoretical understanding and practical application.

- **Boost confidence:** As the hours of dedicated study accumulate and your grasp of the material solidifies, your confidence will naturally grow. The fear of facing the DMV exam will be replaced by assurance in your preparedness, reducing the apprehension that often goes hand in hand with test-taking.
- **Save time:** In the quest for knowledge, time is a precious commodity. Instead of searching through various resources, this handbook consolidates everything you need in one convenient place. Simplify your efforts, channel your focus, and gain time you would have otherwise spent sifting through different materials.
- **Expert advice:** Benefit from the author's experience as a driving instructor, offering insights from practical teaching that enhance your understanding of the rules of the road.
- **Future driving success:** Your ambitions extend beyond the DMV exam; they embrace a future of driving responsibility and safety. As you absorb the wisdom in these pages, you're not just preparing to pass a test but also laying the foundation for a lifetime of conscientious driving habits, ensuring the safety of yourself and others on the road.

In essence, this book is more than just a study tool; it's a companion, mentor, and pathway to your road-ready success. Seize the opportunity, embrace the shortcuts, and embark on a journey that goes beyond exams, shaping a safer, more knowledgeable future behind the wheel.

So, buckle up as we embark together. From basics to nuances, from straightforward to tricky scenarios, this handbook is meticulously crafted to be your ultimate companion. By the final page, you'll not only have the knowledge to ace the DMV exam but also the confidence to navigate roads like a true aficionado.

Get ready to head out on the open road toward the Florida dream—one road sign at a time, one intersection at a time. The journey begins now, and the destination is clear: your license to explore the breathtaking views and vibrant tapestry of The Sunshine State.

As you embark on the enlightening ride through the pages of this handbook, a transformative end result awaits you, one that extends far beyond the confines of a mere driver's exam. Feel the weight of nervous anticipation replaced with the thrill of assured knowledge. Envision yourself navigating the roads of Florida with a newfound sense of mastery, effortlessly interpreting road signs, adhering to right-of-way protocols, and maneuvering complex intersections with an ease you once deemed unattainable.

But what makes the author the proper authority, the best person to guide you on this journey? The answer lies in their extensive experience and unparalleled expertise in the realm of driving instruction. Having spent over a decade educating aspiring drivers and diligently studying the nuances of driving laws, the author stands as a beacon of wisdom and a trusted mentor.

Before this "new" information, the DMV exam posed a formidable hurdle, and understanding Florida's driving laws felt like decoding a cryptic message. Accessible resources were scarce, leading to frustration, uncertainty, and exam failures. Now, with this book, you have a roadmap guiding you through every aspect of the DMV exam. It bridges the gap between inexperience and mastery, breaking down complex topics into digestible segments and illustrating practical applications with real-life scenarios.

Amidst widespread information and anxiety, The Most Complete and Easy-to-Follow Florida DMV Exam Handbook With 250 Practice Questions stands as your beacon of clarity. With insights from an experienced guide, feel assured as you navigate your journey. This isn't just any book—it's the right one for you. With each page turn, you're on the expressway to success, confidence, and skilled, responsible driving.

1

UNDERSTANDING THE LICENSING PROCESSING SYSTEM

D id you know Florida has over 16 million licensed drivers, and thousands of new drivers join this group every year? Here's how they do it.

Becoming a licensed driver in Florida is a significant milestone, symbolizing your path to freedom and independence. This chapter outlines the steps and requirements for acquiring a Florida driver's license, from your visit to the DMV to the issuance of your new license.

As you continue reading, you'll discover valuable information about driving, the rules of the road, and your responsibilities as a licensed driver. It's essential to remember that having a driver's license is a privilege that can be revoked.

So, get ready for this adventure. Let's explore the steps and prepare you to join the ranks of Florida's proud and skilled licensed drivers.

The Florida Department of Motor Vehicles establishes the age requirement for minors, 15 years old, to be eligible to apply for a learner's permit. This permit allows the student driver to practice driving while supervised by a licensed driver at least 21 years old.

The DMV chooses 15 as the minimum age to strike a balance between allowing young individuals to start learning how to drive while ensuring they have reached a level of maturity that promotes responsible and safe driving practices. As you progress in your teenage years, you'll be better equipped to comprehend the intricacies of driving regulations and make well-informed decisions on the road.

Before you arrive at the DMV to apply for your learner's permit, it is best that you have the correct documents in your possession. The DMV requires proof of identity, and the following documents are acceptable: a valid U.S. passport, a certified birth certificate, a Permanent Resident Card (Green Card), or a Consular Report of Birth Abroad.

The DMV requires proof of validity of your social security number (SSN), and the following documents are acceptable: Your Social Security card, a W-2 form, or a pay stub that bears your whole SSN.

The DMV requires two proofs of residency in Florida, and the following documents are acceptable: A utility bill, rental or lease agreement, bank statement, or mortgage statement.

Minors seeking a Learner's permit must provide evidence of the successful completion of a Traffic Law and Substance Abuse Education Course. Accredited driving schools administer the program, and upon its completion, the school issues a certificate of completion to the student.

Prepare for a smooth DMV process at the Florida Department of Motor Vehicles. Ensure you have the correct forms, such as class 'E' for regular vehicles, 'A', 'B' or 'C' for commercial licenses, and a parental consent form for minors. Prioritize accuracy, legibility, and completeness when filling out forms to prevent delays. Double-check details like your name, date of birth, and Social Security number to avoid complications.

Follow instructions for supporting documents and identification numbers. Utilize the Online Appointment System on the official Florida DMV website to schedule your appointment for a smoother process. Ensure you have all the necessary information before booking and arrive promptly to avoid delays. A DMV representative will inspect and authenticate your documents. Note that to do transactions online on the DMV website, you must create a "My DMV Account."

Be confident in the knowledge test; your hard work and preparation, along with the study questions in this book, will make it easier. Be prepared for fingerprinting and a photo for your driver's license. Now that you know the process, gather your documents, complete the forms, schedule your appointment, and stay motivated for your Florida learner's permit.

THE KNOWLEDGE EXAM

The knowledge exam aims to evaluate your knowledge of traffic rules, road signs, and safe driving practices. It ensures you possess the information necessary to navigate the roads safely and responsibly.

Read, take notes, and make sure you truly understand it. But don't stop there. You've got a bank of practice test questions in this book and online at the DMV website (flhsmv.gov). These practice rounds aren't just warm-ups. They offer an opportunity to assess your knowledge and become acquainted with the format of the real exam. Taking these practice tests is not only about understanding the content but also mastering your approach to the exam.

Keep in mind, this phase focuses on the fundamentals of responsible driving. Visualize yourself successfully and accurately answering those questions during the exam. This mental preparation can help alleviate anxiety and get you ready to go.

Speaking of questions, here's what you'll face: Multiple-choice questions. Each question gives you a situation or a question, and you have a set of answers. Your job is simple: Pick the correct answer according to the driving laws and what makes sense on the road.

This book comprehensively covers virtually all exam topics, including right-of-way, speed limits, road sign recognition, and meanings. Don't rush, read questions carefully, and aim for at least 40 correct answers out of 50 for a passing score. Keep in mind that this journey is about more than passing a test; it's about gaining the knowledge for responsible and confident driving in Florida.

THE VISION EXAM

Your eyesight will undergo an examination at the driver's license office. If deemed necessary based on the outcome, you might need to wear corrective lenses while driving. This is required if the lenses enhance your vision, contributing to safer driving. In cases of inconclusive results, a referral to your doctor may be made.

Unlike the written exam, the vision exam doesn't follow a pass/fail scoring system. Instead, it evaluates whether your visual acuity and peripheral vision meet the minimum requirements for safe driving, ensuring you possess the necessary capabilities to navigate the roads responsibly.

Now that you have learned about the exams, it's time to talk about the next phase, which is to practice for the behind-the-wheel exam. For all minors, in addition to having to wait until being 16 years of age, the DMV has a mandatory wait time of 12 months from the issue date of attaining the learner's permit before they are eligible to take the behind-the-wheel test.

All minors are to do 50 hours behind the wheel practice with 10 of those being at night. Be sure to log all the practice hours, a handy log is available at the back of the book. The minor can practice with any licensed driver 21 years or older seated in the front passenger seat.

It's ideal to practice with someone who possesses considerable driving experience, patience, and the capacity to provide constructive feedback. The time spent together should focus on mentorship and guidance, as these aspects greatly influence your driving ability. While not obligatory, enrolling in professional driving lessons from a driving school significantly improves your driving and defensive skills, better preparing you for the behind-the-wheel test.

YOUR PROGRESS CHECKLIST

To help you track your progress to getting your learner's permit and ensure that no step is missed, we've created a comprehensive checklist. Keep this checklist handy and mark each milestone as you achieve it. Let's embark on this journey of preparation and progress together.

Driver Education and Training

[ ] Completed a state-approved driver education program.

Written Test Preparation

[ ] Thoroughly studied the Florida Driver Handbook.

[ ] Have developed an understanding of road signs, traffic rules, and safe driving practices.

[ ] Utilized the practice questions in this book and on the DMV website to assess your knowledge and readiness.

Documentation Collection

[ ] Gathered proof of identity, Social Security number and Florida residency.

[ ] Collected required documentation and supporting materials.

Form Completion

[ ] Filled out the Driver's License or Identification Card Application form accurately and completely.

Appointment Scheduling

[ ] Scheduled a DMV appointment.

Final Preparations

[ ] Double-checked all required documents and paperwork.

[ ] Arranged necessary identification for the DMV visit.

[ ] Ensured familiarity with the DMV location and directions.

DMV Appointment

[ ] Attended the scheduled DMV appointment.

[ ] Presented all required documents and identification.

[ ] Successfully completed any necessary tests or evaluations.

Knowledge Test Success

[ ] Passed the knowledge test.

[ ] Secured a learner's permit.

Behind-The-Wheel Training

[ ] Continued practicing driving skills with the guidance of a licensed driver 21 or older.

[ ] Developed confidence in various driving scenarios, such as city driving, highway navigation, and parking.

Professional Driving Lessons

[ ] Received professional behind the wheel training from a certified Driving School.

Driving Test Preparation

[ ] Developed practical skills for maneuvering the vehicle.

[ ] Gained an understanding of road etiquette and safe driving behavior.

[ ] Practiced parallel parking, three-point turns, and other essential maneuvers.

Driving Test Success

[ ] Passed the driving test.

Obtained Your Driver's License

[ ] Received your driver's license.

As you progress through each stage of the licensing process, utilize this checklist to monitor your accomplishments. This roadmap acts as a visual depiction of your progress and a source of motivation, steering you toward obtaining your Florida driver's license successfully. Every checkmark signifies a step closer to your objective—the day you confidently assume control of the wheel and embrace the privileges and responsibilities of a licensed driver. Stay focused, diligent, and on course as you embark on this exciting new phase of your life. Now that you're acquainted with the steps needed to obtain your driver's license, let's tackle the first significant challenge: understanding Florida's traffic laws.

2

EXPLORING FLORIDA TRAFFIC LAWS

A s you begin your journey to becoming a confident and knowledgeable driver, you must thoroughly understand the rules that govern our roadways. From sun-drenched coastlines to the swamp lands, Florida offers a majestic backdrop for your driving adventures. However, even in the Sunshine State, some "free" things can come with a price tag. Case in point: Have you ever wondered why a Florida driver received a traffic citation at a supposedly free parking lot? The answer lies in the realm of traffic laws.

While you navigate through this comprehensive handbook, you'll gain an in-depth understanding of the regulations that keep our roads safe, the consequences of not following them, and strategies to help you avoid costly pitfalls.

With its diverse landscapes and vibrant cities, Florida offers a variety of driving situations that demand a thorough understanding of traffic regulations. From the bustling streets of Miami to the tranquil high-ways of the Everglades, each region presents its own set of challenges for drivers to navigate. It's vital to approach your driving experience equipped with knowledge that helps you navigate confidently and safe-guards you from unintended citations.

In addition to covering essential driving laws and regulations, we will cover lesser-known ones that could catch even the most experienced drivers off-guard. We'll discuss everything from right-of-way rules to specific speed limits, parking intricacies, and the proper use of turn signals, to name a few. By the time you finish this chapter, you'll have a comprehensive understanding of the rules that contribute to the orderly flow of traffic in Florida. Let's begin this journey through Florida's traffic laws.

IN-DEPTH REVIEW OF THE TRAFFIC LAWS

Basic Road Rules

It's important to know the core principles of Florida's traffic laws. A firm understanding of these principles is essential for safe and responsible driving. Here, we will explore topics that encompass speed limits, right of way, yielding, stopping, and turning rules, among others.

Speed Limits

Speed limits in Florida serve as a protective measure for all road users. These limits vary, accommodating for things like the type of road, surrounding environment, and weather conditions. It's crucial to obey posted speed limits, as excessive speed can result in accidents and traffic violations. Here are the key takeaways:

- When entering any road, look for and follow all the posted speed limits. These limits are carefully determined based on road design, traffic volume, and nearby establishments.

- The Florida Basic Speed Law mandates drivers adjust their speed according to driving conditions, irrespective of the posted speed limit, meaning drivers must reduce their speed to what is safe and reasonable in adverse weather, heavy traffic, or hazardous situations.

Right-Of-Way

Understanding and respecting right-of-way regulations is crucial for insuring smooth traffic flow and prevent collisions. Some things to keep in mind:

- At all-way-stop intersections (every corner has a stop sign), the vehicle that arrives first is granted the right of way. If two vehicles arrive at the intersection simultaneously, the vehicle on the right takes precedence.
- A green light signifies your right to proceed; however, you must yield to pedestrians or vehicles that are still in the intersection.
- A solid yellow light means the intersection is transitioning from a green light to a red light. You, as a driver, must determine if a safe stop is still possible or to continue through the intersection; it is not against the law to enter the intersection while the traffic light remains yellow; it is against the law to enter once the traffic light is red.
- A solid red light means to make a complete stop.

Yielding

Yielding involves granting precedence to other road users before proceeding. This practice is vital to avoiding accidents and maintaining an orderly traffic flow. Key yielding rules include:

- Upon encountering a yield sign, slow down and be prepared to stop for pedestrians and vehicles with the right-of-way.
- At open intersections, the vehicle already in the intersection has the right of way. A vehicle on a state highway supersedes a vehicle from a secondary road, while a vehicle on a paved road supersedes a vehicle from an unpaved road. Additionally, a vehicle going straight has the right of way over a vehicle turning left.
- Pedestrians are to be granted the right of way in both designated and unmarked crosswalks. It is incumbent upon you to stop and allow them to finish crossing safely.

Stops

Making complete stops is not only the law but also greatly improves safety. A complete stop encompasses the vehicle coming to a full motionless position, being behind the limit line, and the driver looking left, right, and left again to confirm it is safe to proceed.

Vital stopping rules encompass:

- Bring your vehicle to a complete stop when approaching a school bus that has flashing red lights and a stop signal arm displayed.
- Whenever you approach a school bus displaying flashing red lights and an extended stop sign, all vehicles must come to a stop, regardless of their direction of travel. Except for vehicles on the opposite side of a road with a raised barrier or an unpaved median at least five feet wide, in which case only the lanes traveling in the direction of the school bus need to stop.

Turning Rules

Making turns in a safe and controlled manner is crucial for the safety of all drivers. Remember the following regarding making turns:

- If no sign prohibits it, making a right turn on a red light is allowed, provided you come to a complete stop and yield the right of way to pedestrians and oncoming traffic.
- When making a left turn, give way to oncoming traffic and pedestrians, and proceed only when it's safe.
- There are protected left turns, meaning you have a green arrow that stops every other driver who could interfere with you as they see a red light on their side of the street. There are "unprotected" left turns; in these turns, the driver gets a green light without an arrow; the opposite side of traffic gets the

same green as you, oncoming traffic, and pedestrians have the right-of-way over the driver making the left turn. It's important to remember that responsible and courteous driving is not just a legal obligation but also a shared duty for all individuals utilizing the roadways.

- Left turns with a flashing yellow arrow means you to yield to oncoming traffic and pedestrians crossing on your left prior to completing the left turn.

PARKING LAWS

A comprehensive grasp of these rules is vital to avoid penalties, maintain traffic flow, and respect the needs of all road users.

Colored Curb Meanings

Colored curbs are strategically employed to convey specific parking restrictions and permissions. Understanding what these curb colors mean is crucial to avoiding parking violations and inconveniences. Here's what you need to know:

- **Red curbs:** Parking is strictly forbidden at red curbs at all times. These zones are reserved for emergency vehicles exclusively, ensuring swift response during emergencies.
- **Yellow curbs:** Yellow curbs indicate loading or unloading zones. Vehicles can briefly stop here to load or unload passengers or goods, with the driver required to stay with the vehicle.
- **Green curbs:** Green curbs allow parking for a limited time; signage typically indicates the time limits drivers must adhere to.
- **White curbs:** A white curb indicates that parking is allowed for picking up or dropping off passengers.
- **Blue curbs:** Blue curbs indicate parking reserved for individuals with disabilities. These reserved parking spaces

play a crucial role in enabling individuals with disabilities to access facilities and services.

Honoring these spaces isn't just a legal obligation but also a reflection of empathy. Here's what you should be aware of:

- **Fines and consequences:** Illegally parking in a handicapped space can result in substantial fines and the potential for your vehicle to get towed.

Parking Scenarios/Distances

Accidents don't solely occur when a vehicle is in motion; an improperly parked vehicle can also lead to a collision. When exiting your vehicle, turn off the engine, engage the parking brake, and take out the key. Prior to opening your car door, make sure to check for approaching traffic behind you. Don't park:

- In front of a driveway.
- Less than 15 feet from a fire hydrant.
- Less than 20 feet from an intersection.
- Less than 30 feet of any traffic control signal such as a stop sign, yield sign or traffic signal.
- Less than 20 feet of a fire station driveway entrance.
- 30 feet of a rural mailbox on a state highway (8 am–6 pm)
- Any place an official sign prohibits it.

Street Cleaning Regulations

Street cleaning is crucial for upholding the cleanliness and appearance of the city's streets. Familiarizing yourself with street cleaning schedules and restrictions is essential to avoid citations or having your vehicle towed. Consider the following:

- **Posted signs:** Pay careful attention to posted signs indicating street cleaning days and times. Parking during these hours can lead to fines or towing.
- **Street sweeper signs:** In certain areas, street cleaning occurs on alternating sides of the street on different days. Ensure you know which side to park on to avoid penalties.

Parking regulations are vital to preserving order on Florida's roads and ensuring equitable access for all road users.

Adhering to these parking laws actively contributes to a more organized and considerate driving environment.

DRIVING UNDER THE INFLUENCE (DUI) LAWS

Learning these laws is essential for maintaining road safety and preventing potentially dangerous situations. We will outline the blood alcohol concentration (BAC) limits and the corresponding penalties associated with DUI offenses in Florida.

Blood Alcohol Concentration Limits

According to Ramos (n.d): "Blood alcohol concentration (BAC) is a measure of the amount of alcohol present in a person's bloodstream". For most drivers in Florida, the legal BAC is:

- **0.08% BAC:** It is illegal for individuals 21 years of age and older to have a BAC of 0.08% or greater and operate a motor vehicle.

For certain groups, stricter BAC limits apply:

- **0.04% BAC:** Commercial drivers operating commercial vehicles are subject to a lower BAC limit of 0.04%.

- **0.02% BAC:** Drivers under the age of 21 are prohibited from operating a motor vehicle with any measurable amount of alcohol in their system; this is commonly referenced as "zero tolerance." A conviction carries an automatic suspension of driving privileges for 6 months.

Penalties for DUI Offenses

Operating a motor vehicle in Florida under the influence of alcohol or drugs is against the law, and the penalties reflect the gravity of the situation. The penalties for DUI can vary based on factors such as prior convictions and the circumstances of the offense. Here is an overview of the potential penalties for offenses:

- **First DUI offense:** A fine of $500 to $1,000 (BAL .15 or higher or minor in the vehicle, not less than $1,000 or more than $2,000), 50 hours of community service, up to 1 year probation, jail time of no more than 6 months (if BAL was at or above .15 or there was a minor in the vehicle then jail time of not more than 9 months), minimum 180 day license revocation, twelve hours of DUI school, a mandatory evaluation to determine if addiction treatment is needed, if court ordered, the use of an Ignition Interlock Device at least six months if BAL at or above .15 or there was a minor in the vehicle.
- **Second DUI offense:** A fine of $1,000 to $2,000 (BAL .15 or higher or minor in the vehicle, not less than $2,000 or more than $4,000), jail time of no more than 9 months, minimum 180-day license revocation, twenty-one hours of DUI school, a mandatory evaluation to determine if addiction treatment is needed, mandated use of an Ignition Interlock Device at least one continuous year.
- **Third DUI offense:** A fine of $2,000 to $5,000 (BAL .15 or higher or minor in the vehicle, not less than $4,000), jail time of no more than 12 months, minimum 180-day license

revocation, twenty-one hours of DUI school, a mandatory evaluation to determine if addiction treatment is needed, mandated use of an Ignition Interlock Device at least two continuous years.

- **Drug related convictions:** According to Florida law, individuals convicted of possessing, selling, or trafficking drugs, including marijuana, will have their driver's license revoked. In addition, if drugs are found in your vehicle because you are utilizing it to transport, sell, or distribute drugs, or to aid in the commission of any other felony, then your car could be seized and forfeited to the arresting agency as contraband.

Understanding Florida's DUI laws for minors and adults as well as the associated penalties is crucial for maintaining road safety and making responsible decisions while operating a motor vehicle. Adhering to the legal BAC limits and avoiding impaired driving safeguards your well-being and protects all road users' safety. It's essential to remember that DUI offenses can have far-reaching consequences, underscoring the importance of making informed and responsible choices behind the wheel.

IMPLICATIONS OF VIOLATING THESE LAWS

Penalties for Traffic Rule Violations

Understanding these penalties is vital for promoting responsible driving behavior, ensuring road safety, and preventing potential legal ramifications. We will provide an in-depth account of the penalties that may follow various traffic rule violations, including fines, points, license suspension, and imprisonment.

Types of Consequences for Traffic Violations

Fines

Fines are a common consequence for traffic violations in Florida. The fine amount can differ depending on which traffic offenses are committed. Some traffic violations, such as exceeding the speed limit or not making complete stops, typically have predetermined fines with fees additionally added by the cities and counties where the violation occurred, while others might be set by a judge based on the circumstances. It's important to note that repeated violations can lead to accumulating fines.

Points on Driving Record

The Florida Department of Motor Vehicles (DMV) operates a point system to track driving infractions (DMV, n.d.). Each traffic violation is assessed as a point value, and these are added to your driving record. Getting an excessive number of points from traffic violations within a specific timeframe can lead to substantial ramifications, such as increased insurance premiums, driver's license suspension, and mandatory attendance to a defensive driving class. The points assigned vary depending on the violation, they range from 3 to 6 points per violation. These points stay on the driving record for three years. Apart from the fines, additional surcharges may be applied to each conviction.

License Suspension

Excessive traffic convictions can lead to license suspension, twelve points within twelve months will lead to a thirty-day suspension, eighteen points within eighteen months will lead to a three month suspension and twenty four points within 36 months will lead to a one year suspension.

Examples of four or more point violations

- Speed > 16 MPH above posted limit – four points
- Exceeding speed limit resulting in a collision – six points
- Not adhering to a traffic signal, sign or device – four points
- Not stopping for a school bus – four points
- Reckless driving – four points
- Texting resulting in a collision – six points

Certain serious traffic violations can result in imprisonment as a penalty. For instance, driving while intoxicated, fleeing the scene of an accident, road rage, or engaging in street racing can lead to incarceration. The length of imprisonment depends on the nature of the offense and whether it is a repeat offense.

INFRACTION–MINOR VIOLATIONS

Infractions are the most common type of traffic violations and are considered minor offenses under Florida law. These violations often result in fines and are typically less severe than the other two categories. Examples of infractions include:

- **Speeding:** Exceeding the posted speed limit.
- **Not stopping at a red light or stop sign:** Disobeying traffic signals.
- **Not making full stops:** Slowing down, but not completely coming to a stop.
- **Not following a sign direction:** Turning right when there is a "no right turn on red sign."
- **Illegal U-Turn:** Making an illegal U-turn where prohibited.
- **Seat belt violation:** Not wearing a seatbelt while driving.
- **Expired registration:** Driving a vehicle with expired registration.
- **Parking violations:** Illegally parking in designated no-parking zones.

Infractions usually carry monetary penalties that vary based on the specific violation. While these violations may not lead to criminal records, they should not be taken lightly, as they contribute to unsafe road conditions and can escalate in fines or consequences against your driver's license if not corrected.

MISDEMEANOR—SERIOUS VIOLATIONS

Misdemeanors are more serious traffic violations that could result in criminal charges. These offenses often involve a higher degree of risk to public safety. Examples of these include:

- **Road Rage:** Aggressive or violent behavior exhibited by a driver on the road.
- **Driving under the influence (DUI):** Operating a motorized vehicle while impaired by alcohol or drugs.
- **Hit and run:** Being involved in a collision and leaving the scene without exchanging necessary information or rendering aid.
- **Driving with a suspended license:** Operating a motorized vehicle despite having a suspended or revoked driver's license.
- **Evading a police officer:** Fleeing from law enforcement in a vehicle.

Consequences for misdemeanors can be fines, probation, community service, and even imprisonment. A conviction for a misdemeanor traffic violation can also result in a criminal record that may affect your current job, future employment opportunities, and other aspects of your life.

FELONY—MAJOR VIOLATIONS

Felony traffic violations are the most severe offenses and carry significant legal consequences due to the substantial risk they pose to public safety. Examples of felony traffic violations include:

- **Vehicular manslaughter:** Causing the death of another person while operating a vehicle recklessly or while intoxicated.
- **Certain DUI offenses:** A DUI that results in the death or serious injury, DUI Manslaughter or a third DUI conviction.
- **Leaving the scene of a fatal accident:** Fleeing the scene of an accident in which a death occurred.
- **Assault with a vehicle:** Using a vehicle as a weapon to harm someone intentionally.

Felony convictions can lead to substantial fines, lengthy prison sentences, and the permanent revocation of driving privileges. The legal and personal consequences of felony traffic violations are severe and far-reaching.

Understanding the categories of traffic violations is essential for all drivers to uphold safety and accountability on Florida's roads. Whether it's an infraction, a misdemeanor, or a felony, it is every driver's responsibility to adhere to the rules of the road and prioritize the well-being of all those sharing the road with them. By familiarizing ourselves with these distinctions, we create a safer and more orderly driving environment for everyone.

Staying up to date with traffic regulations helps ensure that you always comply with the law and, most importantly, drive safely with others on the road.

HOW TO STAY INFORMED ABOUT CHANGES IN LAWS

The DMV Website (flhsmv.gov): Your Trustworthy Guide

The Florida DMV website is a crucial resource for driving regulations, road safety, and legal requirements. Regularly visiting this official platform is highly recommended to stay informed about any changes to traffic laws. The DMV website, maintained by state authorities, is your reliable source for accurate and up-to-date information on Florida traffic laws. Amendments are promptly updated, ensuring quick access to changes that may impact your driving habits.

Local News: Your Window to Community Changes

Local news outlets, spanning newspapers, TV, radio, and online platforms, are vital for keeping communities informed. They cover topics like traffic laws, including updates on signs, speed limits, and road closures, directly impacting residents' daily commutes and driving experience.

EXPLORING FLORIDA TRAFFIC LAWS—SELF-ASSESSMENT QUIZ

Test your understanding of Florida traffic laws with the following multiple-choice and true/false questions based on the laws discussed in this chapter. Choose the best answer for each question.

Multiple Choice

1. A DUI conviction can carry a consequence of:

  a) A fine.
  b) Driver License suspension.
  c) Jail time.
  d) All of the above.

2. Traffic Violations:

a) Carry monetary fines.

b) Add points to the driving record.

c) Both a and b.

d) Are only monetary fines, no points are added to the driving record.

3. This is not a traffic violation:

a) Not taking a shopping cart to the designated shopping cart area after shopping.

b) Driving 10 miles above the speed limit.

c) Not stopping for a red light.

d) Not stopping at a stop sign.

4. Which of the following BAC levels is illegal if under 21:

a) .08.

b) .04.

c) .02.

d) All of the above.

True/False

5. True or False: Texting that results in a collision is a three-point violation.

6. True or False: A first DUI offence may carry a six-month prison sentence.

7. True or False: A speeding citation of ten miles over the speed limit is a three-point violation.

8. True or False: To stay safe from citations and follow Florida's traffic laws it's good enough to follow what everyone else does.

Answers
Multiple Choice
d)c)a)d)
True/False
FTTF

3

COMMON SENSE RULES OF THE ROAD

"The way I drive, the way I handle a car, is an expression of my inner feelings."

— LEWIS HAMILTON

Florida's diverse and ever-changing roadways demand more than just following regulations; they require a nuanced understanding of the unspoken language of traffic flow. Within these pages, we'll uncover the unwritten rules facilitating interaction between vehicles, pedestrians, and cyclists. More than memorizing right-of-way protocols, we'll explore the essence of yielding and the importance of maintaining a safety cushion of space for unforeseen situations.

This chapter is about embracing the responsibility that comes with being behind the wheel and realizing that your choices influence your safety and those around you. Manners are more than a formality; you'll learn the power of patience and the generosity of allowing others to merge during peak traffic hours.

Approach the following sections with an open mind and readiness to absorb. By embracing the fundamental principles of common sense and politeness on Florida roads, you elevate your driving standard. Let's embark on this journey to become a proficient, respectful, and exceptional driver on Florida's vibrant roads.

ESSENTIAL MANNERS FOR FLORIDA DRIVERS

Understanding Lane Purpose

While navigating Florida's highways and byways, understanding drivers' speeds according to their lanes is crucial. The right lane, often called the "slow lane," is vital for orderly traffic flow. It's meant for vehicles traveling at a moderate pace, contrasting with the left lanes, known as the "fast lane."

The Overtaking Rule

One of the critical aspects of driving in the right lane is overtaking slower-moving vehicles. While the right lane is for steady cruising, maintaining traffic flow is crucial for safety. If you encounter a slower vehicle ahead, instead of urging the driver to speed up, pass them safely by moving into the left lane and returning to the right lane promptly to keep traffic flowing smoothly.

Enhancing Traffic Flow and Safety

Efficient traffic flow depends on vehicles staying in their lanes. Slower vehicles on the right help faster traffic move smoothly, reducing congestion and minimizing sudden lane changes. Safety is the essence of proper lane discipline, especially in the right lane where exits, ramps, and merging traffic occur. Staying in this lane when not passing enables better handling of these situations, reduces traffic disruption, and provides a buffer for entering vehicles, lowering collision risks.

Exceptions and Flexibility

Exceptions exist to every rule. In heavy traffic or adverse conditions, staying in the right lane may be necessary. Safety remains of upmost importance, but if consistently passing vehicles, briefly switching to the left lane is appropriate. On single-lane highways, slower drivers must promptly pull over to the right to ease congestion.

Courtesy to Pedestrians—Respecting the Right-Of-Way

It's important to remember that drivers share the road with other drivers, motorcyclists, bicyclists, and, most notably, pedestrians, who have the least protection if involved in a traffic collision.

Pedestrians and Their Priority

Pedestrians are the most vulnerable participants in the traffic equation; therefore, drivers are to give pedestrians the right-of-way at crosswalks or intersections. Additionally, drivers must do their best to stop and give the right-of-way if a pedestrian crosses at unexpected areas, such as mid-block. As a driver, you have a legal and ethical obligation to yield to pedestrians in these scenarios. Adhering to this rule promotes road safety and contributes to a more considerate and harmonious driving culture.

Vigilance at Crosswalks and intersections

Marked crosswalks serve as visual indicators for drivers to anticipate pedestrian activity. Approach crosswalks—whether at an intersection or mid-block—with added vigilance. Be ready to yield to pedestrians waiting or crossing. Prioritizing pedestrian safety is crucial. Intersections, where driver and pedestrian paths intersect, demand increased attention for pedestrian safety. This is particularly important during turns, especially right turns, where you must ensure that your path is clear of any crossing pedestrians before proceeding, remember pedestrians have the right of way until the crosswalk is clear; drivers must exercise patience and remain stopped until this occurs.

School Zones and Pedestrian Hotspots

Areas around schools, parks, and other recreational spaces are pedestrian hotspots. These zones demand extra vigilance and slower speeds, as they are likely to be frequented by children and families. Anticipate the unexpected and be prepared to yield to pedestrians, particularly children who might not sense the danger and cross unexpectedly.

Shared Spaces and Unmarked Crossing

It's important to know that pedestrians' right of way isn't confined solely to marked crosswalks; but rather to all shared spaces, parking lots, or areas without marked crossings. Drivers should anticipate pedestrians' movements and give them the space to navigate safely.

Use of Turn Signals—A Precursor to Safe Maneuvers

Communication is critical to seamless movement in the intricate dance of traffic. This chapter unveils an essential aspect of responsible driving—using turn signals well in advance to prevent mishaps and ensure a harmonious flow on Florida's roads.

Signaling Intentions

Turn signals—those seemingly simple blinking lights on your vehicle —carry a hefty responsibility. They serve as your voice on the road, conveying your intentions to fellow drivers; it can imply a lane change, a turn, or even a merge. By utilizing turn signals effectively, you're ensuring that drivers around you are aware of your intention well before executing them.

The Importance of Timing

The key to appropriately using turn signals lies in the timing of when they are used; for instance, using your turn signal a split second before turning does little to inform other drivers of your intentions. Instead, develop a habit of turning on your turn signal well in advance. The Florida Vehicle Code requires a minimum of 100 feet before your intended maneuver (DMV, n.d.); thus allowing other drivers to adjust their speeds and positions, preventing late reactions and potential collisions.

Lane Changes Made Clear

Changing lanes is a prime example of when using your turn signal is critical. It's not just about signaling your intention; it's about ensuring the space you're moving into is available and safe. Before completing a lane change:

- Activate your turn signal.
- Check your side and rear mirror and look over your shoulder to confirm there is nothing in your blind spot.
- Confidently complete your lane change.

This sequence of actions optimizes safety for you and your fellow drivers.

Merging With Finesse

Turn signals must be used when merging onto freeways. This action allows drivers in adjacent lanes to make room for you or maintain their speed, allowing for safe merging onto the freeways.

Turn Signal Does Not Equal Right-Of-Way

While turn signals signify intent, it's important to remember that they don't grant you the right-of-way; you must still verify if it is safe to proceed with your maneuver.

Preventing Confusion and Mishaps

The core purpose of using turn signals well in advance is to prevent confusion. By clearly communicating your intentions, you reduce the risk of misunderstandings that can lead to sudden braking, swerving, or collisions.

EXPLORING THE IMPORTANCE OF RESPECTING OTHER DRIVERS ON THE ROAD

Distracted Driving—Navigating the Perils of Inattention

The Lure of Distraction

The allure of a ringing phone or a blinking screen can be difficult to ignore. But while driving, a momentary distraction can have grave repercussions. Whether viewing a text, typing a reply, or simply checking an app, even a few seconds of distraction from the road can lead to disastrous outcomes.

The Cognitive Burden

Distracted driving extends beyond visual distractions—it involves a cognitive load that takes attention from driving safely. Texting, especially, demands mental focus crucial for being a safe driver—assessing surroundings, anticipating hazards, and making quick decisions. Shifting attention between driving and a device impairs reaction to unexpected situations. Cell phones require visual and manual attention, turning even brief distractions into potential collisions. This mental disconnect, often referred to as "tunnel vision," can cause delayed responses, making it challenging to avoid hazards.

The Human Toll

Distracted driving has far-reaching consequences, causing injuries, deaths, and lasting emotional distress. A momentary lapse in focus can alter lives permanently. Responsible drivers prioritize safety, committing to stay focused and mitigate harm. Disable notifications, secure your phone, and avoid distractions while driving. Urgent calls or messages can wait—safety cannot.

Road Rage—Navigating Stressful Situations With Composure

Being on the road can be challenging: Temperaments can escalate, and stress can run high. In this chapter, we delve into a scenario that affects every driver at some point: road rage. As responsible drivers on Florida's roads, maintaining composure under pres-  sure and avoiding confrontations is paramount for safe and harmonious driving.

Understanding the Trigger and Keeping Cool

Road rage often arises from stressors such as traffic and personal frustrations, leading to angry outbursts. Allowing these emotions to control your behavior on the road can escalate situations and compromise safety. Responding to road rage with aggression fosters hostility and danger. Small gestures or insults can quickly turn into dangerous situations. Stay composed, focus on your destination, and manage anger without letting it control you. Cultivate a calm mindset for responsible driving.

Make avoiding confrontations a guiding principle while driving. If encountering an aggressive driver, refrain from reacting aggressively. Avoid eye contact, distance yourself, and let them continue. Remember, a sign of strength is to disengage.

De-escalation Techniques

If you find yourself dealing with an angry driver, consider employing de-escalation techniques. If you made a mistake, accept it with a nod of acknowledgment, rather than an aggressive gesture, it could defuse tension. Similarly, allowing an impatient driver to merge in front of you can lower their frustration, making it a more positive driving setting.

Report, Don't Retaliate

If you encounter an angry driver, do your best to avoid confrontation, maintain distance, and report incidents if necessary. Stay composed to diffuse tension and prioritize safety for yourself and others on the road. Confront road rage with patience and restraint, displaying maturity, respect, and a commitment to shared safety. By avoiding confrontations, you contribute to a collective effort that transforms the road into a space where courtesy, empathy, and safety prevail.

HOW TO APPLY COMMON SENSE WHILE DRIVING

Following the Speed Limit—A Journey in Safe Pace

Designed for Safety

Speed limits are not arbitrarily set; they are established after carefully considering various factors, including road design, traffic flow, and pedestrian activity. Roads are designed to accommodate specific speeds, considering factors like curves, intersections, and potential hazards. Following speed limits contributes to a safer road experience for yourself and others.

A Buffer for Reaction Time

Driving within the speed limit allows for adequate time to perceive hazards, make decisions, and react appropriately. Exceeding the speed limit reduces this reaction time, increasing the risk of accidents when unexpected events occur, such as sudden lane changes or obstacles on the road.

The Myth of Empty Roads

Even on empty roads, following the speed limit is crucial. Unforeseen situations like pedestrians, animals, or emerging vehicles can occur suddenly. Speeding reduces your ability to react promptly and safely to these situations.

Fuel Efficiency and Emissions

Adhering to speed limits enhances safety and contributes to lower fuel consumption and reduced emissions. By driving at a controlled pace, you're making an environmentally conscious choice.

Driving According to Weather Conditions—Adapting for Safety

Rain and Reduced Traction

When rain graces the roads, the water on the road reduces traction between your tires and the surface, leading to longer stopping distances and a higher risk of skidding. This is especially true after a dry spell; the road can become slippery due to accumulated  lubricants and impurities. To stay safe in the rain, slow down, increase your following distance, brake gently, use headlights for visibility, and avoid sudden maneuvers.

Fog and Limited Visibility

Fog can transform familiar roads into treacherous terrains of limited visibility. Under these circumstances, slow down and use your low-beam headlights or fog lights for increased visibility to other drivers. Maintain a safe distance from the vehicle you're following and don't use high beams, as they can contribute to decreased visibility by reflecting off the fog the fog.

Snow and Ice

When driving in areas of snow and ice, the golden rule is to decrease your speed. Snow and ice drastically reduce your tires' traction, making it easier to lose control. Accelerate, brake, and turn gently to avoid skids. Increase your following distance to allow yourself sufficient time to react. If your vehicle starts skidding, steer gently in the direction you want to go, and don't turn the steering wheel abruptly.

Strong Winds and Crosswinds

Wind can be a formidable force on the road, particularly on highways and open spaces. When driving in areas of strong winds or crosswinds, maintain a firm grip on the steering wheel and anticipate abrupt gusts that can push your vehicle off course. When passing large vehicles, slow down and stay alert, as they can create wind turbulence.

Hot Weather and Tire Health

High temperatures can impact your tires' health, leading to blowouts. Inspect the pressure on your tires regularly since heat can lead to increased tire pressure. Avoid overinflating your vehicle's tires, as this can further stress your tires. If you experience a blowout, keep a steady grip on the wheel, gradually decelerate, and pull over to a safe location.

Adapting to Unpredictable Conditions

Weather conditions can change quickly, especially in Florida's varied climate zones. Check the weather forecast up to and right before starting any trip. If conditions worsen during your drive, consider pulling over at a safe location, such as a rest area, continue once conditions improve.

Adapting to weather conditions is essential for safe driving. By doing so, you prioritize safety, minimize risks, and contribute to road harmony. These lessons, including yielding to pedestrians, using turn signals, and staying cool under pressure are fundamental for safe road navigation.

Now, armed with a comprehensive understanding of courteous and attentive driving, let's transition into the next phase of our exploration —the realm of road signs. As we delve into the world of road signs, you'll discover how these symbols communicate crucial information, from speed limits to potential hazards.

QUESTIONNAIRE

Let's put your newfound knowledge of common sense rules to the test with some scenario-based questions. Consider each situation carefully and choose the option that aligns best with responsible and considerate driving.

Remember, the choices you make while driving impact your safety and the safety of others. Take your time to consider each scenario and select the option that aligns with responsible and courteous driving practices. Your commitment to applying common sense rules on the road contributes to a safer and more harmonious driving experience for everyone.

Scenario 1: Speed Limits

What factors are taken into account to develop speed limits?

a) Road design, traffic flow, and pedestrian activity.
b) The age and size of the vehicles that will travel on the road.
c) The meaning of the name of the road.

Scenario 2: Using Turn Signals

You find yourself in heavy traffic and need to change lanes. What should you do?

a) Activate the turn signal and initiate the lane change immediately; the other drivers must yield the right of way to you.
b) Activate your turn signal, sound your horn at least twice, and swiftly switch lanes.
c) Activate your turn signal well in advance, check your mirrors, look over your shoulder, and complete the lane change when it's safe.

Scenario 3: Road Rage

Another driver is tailgating you and honking aggressively. It's best to:

a) Use your brakes abruptly to teach them a lesson.
b) Stay calm, maintain your speed, and let them pass when it's safe.
c) Gesture or shout back at them.

Scenario 4: Following the Speed Limit

You're driving on an empty road where you don't see any other vehicles around. What should you do?

a) Go as fast as you feel it's safe; empty roads are not subject to specific speed limits per the Florida Vehicle Code.
b) Maintain a speed slightly above the limit, as there's no traffic.
c) Adhere to the posted speed limit, regardless of the absence of other vehicles.

Scenario 5: Adapting to Weather Conditions

Heavy rain has started after a lengthy dry spell, reducing visibility and creating slippery roads. How would you adjust the way you drive?

a) Maintain your typical speed; the first 30 minutes after a dry spell are the safest when it rains.
b) Speed up to arrive at your destination quicker.
c) Slow down and exercise additional caution; the first 30 minutes of rain after a dry spell can be especially slippery. Increase the following distance and use headlights to enhance visibility.

Scenario 6: Distracted Driving

You receive a text message while driving. What's the best course of action?

a) Pull over to the side of the road to respond safely.
b) Read and reply to the message while keeping an eye on the road.
c) Respond to the message quickly while waiting at a red light.

Scenario 7: Right Lane Discipline

You're driving on a multilane road. What's the primary purpose of the right lane?

a) It's meant for high-speed driving and overtaking slower vehicles.
b) It's designated for parked vehicles and is not meant for driving.
c) It's a lane to cruise at a moderate pace, allowing smoother traffic flow.

Scenario 8: Courtesy to Pedestrians

You're approaching an intersection to turn right; a pedestrian is ready to cross the crosswalk. What should you do?

a) Speed through the turn, the pedestrian has lost the right of way by not being proactive and started crossing.
b) Stop completely before the crosswalk, ensuring the pedestrian can cross safely.
c) Slow down slightly but continue the turn without stopping for pedestrians to avoid being rear-ended.

Scenario 9: Merging Onto Highways

You're merging onto a busy highway. How should you enter the traffic flow?

a) Activate your turn signal, adjust your speed to that of the traffic flow, and merge safely into a gap.
b) Bring the vehicle to a complete and sudden stop.
c) Speed up and force your way into a gap; if necessary, lower your window and give a hand gesture to let the other driver know you are going in.

Scenario 10: Planning

Before starting a long road trip, it's a good idea to?

a) Stay up late as much as possible, you can recover on the long drive.
b) Check weather conditions for the entirety of the road trip.
c) Leave a few minutes behind schedule to challenge yourself to make up the time along the way.

Answers
1-a 2-c 3-b 4-c 5-c 6-a 7-c 8-b 9-a 10-b

4

UNDERSTANDING ROAD SIGNS

R oad signs serve as silent guides on the road, providing crucial information, warnings, and instructions to drivers. As you progress through this chapter, you'll learn about various types of road signs, from regulatory and warning signs to guide and informational signs. Our approach is both practical and objective, aimed at preparing you to identify these signs effortlessly and respond appropriately in real-life driving scenarios.

Understanding road signs is crucial for driver safety, serving as a universal language that transcends language barriers. It's not only essential for obtaining your driver's license but also vital for ensuring your safety and that of others on the road.

Upon finalizing this chapter, you will know how to

- **Identify road signs:** You will become well-versed in recognizing the distinct shapes, colors, symbols, and messages associated with each type of road sign. This ability is important to make quick and accurate decisions while driving.

- **Decode their meanings:** We will explore the meanings of various categories of road signs, ranging from regulatory signs such as stop signs, which require a complete stop, to speed limit signs indicating safe driving speeds, and caution signs warning of potential hazards.
- **Prepare for real-life driving:** Our objective is to ensure your success on the DMV test and equip you for safe and competent driving in real-life situations. These road signs are not just theoretical concepts; they are tools designed to facilitate safe and responsible driving.

Remember, this chapter isn't just about memorizing; it's about understanding and applying the rationale behind road signs to your driving.

COMPREHENSIVE GUIDE TO ROAD SIGNS

Road signs are the essential language of the road, providing crucial information to drivers. For easy recognition and understanding, let's break down these signs by shape, color, and symbols.

Regulatory Signs

When you encounter them, you must adhere to their instructions without exception. These signs often indicate restrictions or actions you must take.

Shape: Regulatory signs are typically rectangular or circular with varying widths. The longer direction is horizontal.

Color: These signs are white with black or red letters and symbols.

Symbols: Examples include

- **Do not enter sign:** A white horizontal bar within a red circle. This sign signifies that you are prohibited from entering the road or lane.

Warning Signs

These signs demand heightened atten-tion and precaution, be sure to adjust your driving accordingly to navigate these hazards safely.

Shape: Warning signs usually have a diamond shape.

Color: These signs are yellow with black symbols and borders.

Symbols: Examples include

- **Curve ahead sign:** Depicts a curving arrow indicating an upcoming curve in the road.
- **Deer crossing sign:** Features an image of a leaping deer, which warns of potential animal crossings.
- **Slippery when wet sign:** Depicts a car skidding on wavy lines. This sign alerts drivers to potentially slippery road conditions when wet.

Guide and Informational Signs

These signs serve as your road companions, assisting you in making informed decisions.

Shape: These signs vary in shape, often rectangular or square.

Color: Guide and informational signs are typically green, blue, or brown with white letters and symbols.

Symbols: Examples include

- **Hospital sign:** Depicts a white "H" on a blue background, indicating nearby medical facilities.
- **Service signs:** Display white symbols on blue backgrounds, indicating services such as rest areas, gas stations, or food.
- **Recreational area sign:** White symbols on brown backgrounds that indicate nearby recreational facilities.

UNDERSTANDING ACTIONS

Let's break down the actions each road sign demands, ensuring you're well-prepared for the diverse scenarios you'll encounter.

STOP Sign

When you encounter a STOP sign, it's non-negotiable. You must come to a complete stop before crossing the limit line; when no limit line is present, then stop before entering the intersection. Ensure the way is clear, and only proceed when it's safe to do so. For maximum safety, please be alert that many drivers treat stop signs

as yield signs and do "slow rolls" or a mere tap on the brakes and continue without coming to a complete stop.

YIELD Sign

A YIELD sign mandates that you yield the right-of-way, and although a full stop isn't mandated, you must reduce your speed and be ready to stop if necessary to give the right-of-way.

"NO" Signs

These signs, usually circular with a red border and a black symbol or text, indicate prohibited actions. When you see a "NO" road sign, the action depicted within the road sign is not permitted.

No U-Turn Sign

When you come across a "NO U-Turn" sign, it's clear: making a U-turn at that point is prohibited. Not respecting this sign can result in a collision with another driver or harm a pedestrian; keep driving and perform the U-turn at a place where it's legal to do so.

No Left Turn Sign

A "NO Left Turn" sign is clear. It means you are not allowed to make a left turn at the indicated location. Plan your route accordingly to avoid left turns where this sign is present.

No Right Turn Sign

Similar to the "NO Left Turn" sign, the "NO Right Turn" sign prohibits making a right turn at the specified location. Abide by this sign's instruction and find an appropriate place to turn right.

No Right Turn on Red Sign

Right turns are permitted only when the light is green. You must wait for the light to turn green before making a right turn, regardless of whether you consider it safe.

School Signs

School signs advise drivers of the presence of a school zone. These signs indicate reduced speed limits when children are likely to be present. Be prepared to slow down and exercise heightened caution in these areas.

Railroad Crossing Signs

When you encounter a railroad crossing sign, it signifies an upcoming railroad crossing. Slow down, prepare to stop if necessary, and ensure the tracks are clear before proceeding. Note that if stopping is required due to an approaching train, you must stop no less than 15 feet but not farther than 50 feet from the railroad track.

CHANGES IN ROAD SIGNS

REDUCED SPEED AHEAD

Drivers must remain up-to-date on road sign changes. Not doing so jeopardizes their overall safety; local news media and the Florida Department of Motor Vehicles website are good sources of information to stay current on road sign changes.

Evolving Road Conditions

Roads are constantly evolving, from construction and expansion projects to changes in traffic flow patterns. As a result, the need for effective communication with drivers becomes paramount. New or temporary road signs are typically used in these scenarios to ensure that drivers remain safe.

Advances in Traffic Management

Traffic management techniques and technologies are in a constant state of evolution; therefore, new road signs might be introduced to improve overall road safety and optimize traffic flow.

Addressing Safety Concerns

The primary purpose of road signs is safety. Suppose authorities identify areas with higher accident rates or specific safety concerns. In that case, they might introduce new road signs or modify existing ones to mitigate risks and prevent accidents.

Legal and Regulatory Changes

Traffic laws and regulations are subject to change over time. Therefore, new road signs are typically used to keep drivers informed about these changes, assuring drivers are up-to-date with their rights and responsibilities.

Urban Planning and Development

Urban planning and development can lead to changes in traffic patterns. New signs may be introduced to guide drivers through newly developed areas, directing them to essential services and ensuring smooth navigation.

THE ADVANTAGES OF TRAFFIC SIGNS

Clear Communication

Road signs provide a standardized and clear way to communicate essential information to drivers. Whether it's indicating speed limits, guiding through complex intersections, or warning about hazards, signs ensure that drivers receive crucial information at a glance.

Universal Language

Road signs transcend language barriers. They provide a universal language that all drivers can understand, regardless of their native language, ensuring consistent communication across diverse communities.

Enhancing Predictability

Consistent road signs enhance predictability for drivers. When drivers know what to expect, they can make informed decisions, reducing the likelihood of abrupt maneuvers or collisions and increasing overall road safety.

Supporting Decision-Making

Traffic signs assist drivers in making quick decisions on the road. They provide timely information about speed limits, directions, potential hazards, and more, empowering drivers to navigate complex situations confidently.

Promoting Order and Safety

Road signs guide drivers, set expectations, and promote orderly traffic flow, reducing accident risks and fostering safe driving behavior. They create a standardized environment that prioritizes safety.

Drivers must understand that road signs evolve to meet changing roadway demands, enhancing overall safety. Staying updated through resources like the official Florida DMV handbook and official websites is crucial, demonstrating a commitment to responsible driving.

Understanding why road signs are essential goes beyond the DMV test —it's about fostering responsible and conscientious driving habits that contribute to the well-being of all road users.

Fundamentally, road signs enhance safety in diverse societies like Florida by providing crucial information, facilitating hazard anticipation, and ensuring orderly traffic flow. They communicate speed limits, right-of-way rules, and directional guidance, reducing confusion and conflicts.

In summary, road signs offer standardized communication, aiding drivers in reaching destinations safely, enhancing predictability, and contributing to a stable driving environment.

NEWS AND MEDIA

Staying updated on road sign changes is vital for drivers. While the basics remain consistent, updates can occur for various reasons, including safety improvements, legal amendments, and advancements in traffic management.

New regulations or legal amendments can prompt changes in road signs. Keeping informed through credible sources enhances safety and driving proficiency.

We've decoded various road signs, understanding their shapes, colors, symbols, and messages. Recognizing their dynamic nature, it's time to apply this knowledge. Every road sign serves a safety purpose, so vigilantly observe and respond while driving, ensuring road orderliness and safety extend beyond passing your DMV test.

As we move on to the next chapter, "Best Driving Practices," consider this a continuation of your journey toward becoming a proficient and responsible driver. So, get ready to explore the principles that will guide you through the intricacies of real-life driving scenarios.

QUESTIONNAIRE

To solidify your understanding of road signs, let's put your knowledge to the test with some practice questions. Get ready to challenge yourself and enhance your road sign recognition skills.

1. A "STOP" sign requires you to:

  a) Stop completely.
  b) Lower speed and proceed with caution.
  c) Give the right-of-way to other vehicles.
  d) Turn left at the intersection.

2. What does a "YIELD" sign mean?

  a) The right-of-way is yours.
  b) Come to a stop.
  c) Reduce speed and, if needed, stop to give the right of way.
  d) Proceed without any restrictions.

3. What does a round "NO U-Turn" sign signify?

  a) You can make a U-turn ahead.
  b) A U-turn is not allowed.
  c) U-turns are allowed only during specific hours.

d) U-turns are permitted, provided there is no oncoming traffic within 200 feet.

4. A sign that is blue with a white "H" signifies?

a) Nearby gas station.
b) Upcoming school zone.
c) Rest area ahead.
d) Nearby medical facility or hospital.

5. Signs that are yellow diamond-shaped typically indicate?

a) Speed limits for the area.
b) Upcoming hazards or warnings.
c) Directional guidance to nearby cities.
d) Locations of recreational areas.

True/False

6. True or False: A right on red is allowed with a "no right on red sign" as long as you have clear visibility for 200 feet.

7. True or False: As you approach a railroad crossing, the flashers are red, you must stop behind the white dynamic envelope "X" markings on the floor.

8. True or False: You should be on heightened alert during dawn if you see a yellow sign with a deer on it.

9. True or False: You can relax a bit and just concentrate on the speed limit on empty roads.

Keep up the great work! In the next chapter, we'll delve into "Best Driving Practices," building on the foundation you've established here and helping you navigate real-life driving situations with confidence and competence.

AnswersTrue/False
1. a) 2. c) 3. b) 4. d) 5. b) 6) F 7) T 8) T 9) F

5

BEST DRIVING PRACTICES

"It is amazing how many drivers, even at the Formula One level, think that the brakes are for slowing the car down."

— MARIO ANDRETTI

J ust like Andretti said, by using the brakes to slow the car down, it allows the driver better control of the vehicle.

This guidebook has given you a solid foundation of knowledge about the rules and regulations that govern our roads. Now, it's time to delve into the heart of responsible and safe driving—the realm of best driving practices.

It's time to delve into the essence of driving, which extends beyond mere rules. It's about grasping the intricacies of the road, recognizing its varied conditions, and adjusting your driving accordingly to prioritize safety for yourself and others. Driving isn't just about mechanical proficiency; it requires a mindful approach that accounts for the constantly shifting dynamics of the road and weather.

Driving is an activity that demands not just knowing how to operate a vehicle—it requires a profound comprehension to treat the road as a living entity. You see, traffic patterns shift, pedestrians emerge, weather conditions change, and unexpected situations unfold. The synergy between your skill as a driver and your ability to adapt will define your success on the road.

This chapter goes beyond the DMV exam to impart practical wisdom and foster good driving habits. We aim to equip you with the confidence to navigate various scenarios safely, ensuring the well-being of all road users. Join us on this enlightening journey to master driving practices that will benefit you on Florida's roads and beyond.

GOOD DRIVING HABITS

It's crucial to understand that the nuances of the road extend far beyond staying between the lines on the pavement or following the speed limits. It's the small, consistent habits that truly make a difference in ensuring not only your safety but also the safety of those around you.

Maintaining a Safe Following Distance

Vehicles need room to maneuver safely. One of the most fundamental habits to adopt is maintaining a safe following distance—a buffer zone between you and the vehicle ahead of you. This space provides you with precious moments to react should the unexpected occur.

The recommended following distance is four seconds in optimal weather and clear visibility. To check if you are maintaining a safe following distance. Pick a stationary object on the road ahead and count the seconds it takes for your vehicle to reach it after the vehicle in front of you passes it. If you find you are not adhering to the recommended following distance, increase your following distance to allow for adequate response time. This distance should be increased based on road conditions and weather (DMV, 2019).

Checking Blind Spots: The Hidden Dangers

Blind spots are areas outside your immediate vision where vehicles or motorcyclists may hide unseen. It's crucial to check your blind spots before changing lanes or making a turn. Before maneuvering, carefully glance over your shoulder to ensure no vehicle is lurking in your blind spot. While mirrors are helpful, they don't show everything. A deliberate check can prevent collisions and avoid surprises.

USING TURN SIGNALS CORRECTLY: COMMUNICATING INTENT

Turn signals are your voice on the road, conveying your intentions to fellow drivers. Using them correctly enhances predictability and reduces confusion. No matter if you're changing lanes, merging onto a highway, or making a turn, remember to signal your intentions well in advance, you must signal at least 100 feet before a turn.

SAFETY GUIDELINES FOR DRIVING ON FLORIDA'S BUSY HIGHWAYS: DRIVING WITH CONFIDENCE

Driving in the bustling landscape of Florida's highways requires a unique blend of skill, alertness, and adaptability.

Maintain a Smooth and Consistent Speed

On Florida's highways, traffic often fluctuates like tides. To ensure a safe journey, aim to maintain a smooth, consistent speed. Abrupt changes in velocity can lead to unnecessary braking, triggering a chain reaction of slowdowns.

Use Your Mirrors Vigilantly

Your mirrors are your allies on the highway— offering a broader view of your surroundings. Adjust them before you start driving and check them regularly. However, remember they don't capture everything. A quick glance over your shoulder, as mentioned earlier, provides a prudent double-check before changing lanes.

Anticipate Traffic Flow

Florida highways can quickly shift from free-flowing to congested. Anticipating traffic flow is a skill honed through experience. Watch for signs of slowing ahead and ease off the accelerator early for smooth deceleration. This proactive approach minimizes sudden braking and enhances safety for all.

Merge With Caution

 Merging onto a busy highway requires cooperation. Signal early, match speed with traffic, and find a suitable gap to merge. Enter smoothly without disrupting traffic, yielding to vehicles already on the highway.

Prepare for Weather Variability

In Florida's diverse climate, expect various weather conditions. Adapt by adjusting your driving for reduced visibility, slippery roads, and longer stopping distances during rain or shine.

By mastering these good driving habits, you're refining your skills and nurturing a sense of responsibility with every mile. The road is a shared space, and through these habits, we build a community of conscientious drivers. As you internalize these practices, you'll embody safe, courteous, and confident driving, going beyond just passing a test.

ADAPTING TO WEATHER

In Florida, weather plays a significant role; various weather conditions require adaptability and vigilance. Let's explore the art of adapting to different weather conditions. This skill ensures your safety and preserves the well-being of everyone sharing the road.

Fog: Peering Through the Mist

Fog can obscure your surroundings, it's crucial to adjust your driving behavior to ensure a safe journey by doing the following:

- **Reduce speed:** Gradually slow-down in accordance with your visibility. Fog impairs distance perception, and driving slower allows you to see better through the fog, giving you more time to react to sudden obstacles.

- **Use low-beam headlights:** Switch on your low-beam headlights to improve your visibility while minimizing glare. High beams typically reflect off the fog, causing reduced visibility.
- **Increase following distance:** Give yourself more than the four second following distance depending on your speed to see stopped vehicles or hazards more quickly as they emerge through the fog. The fog may mask brake lights, requiring extra time for a safe stop.
- **Stay cautious at intersections:** Approach intersections with extreme caution. Cross-traffic might be challenging to see; therefore, reduce speed and be prepared to yield or stop if necessary.

Rain: Navigating Slippery Slopes

Rain can transform roadways into slick surfaces, testing your ability to maintain control and awareness. To navigate rainy conditions safely, consider these strategies:

- **Turn on headlights:** Rain decreases visibility, so turn on your headlights to enhance your visibility and make your vehicle more visible to others.
- **Increase following distance:** Stopping distance increases in the rain. Make sure to maintain a larger-than-normal following distance between you and the car ahead to allow ample braking time.
- **Smooth and gentle maneuvers:** Sudden maneuvers can lead to skidding. Brake, accelerate, and steer gently to maintain control. Think of how you walk when the sidewalk is wet; you are more careful not to make any sudden maneuvers that may cause you to slip and fall, correct? Apply the same common sense for driving in the rain.

- **Watch for hydroplaning:** When water accumulates on the road's surface, your tires can lose contact with the pavement, leading to hydroplaning. If this happens, ease off the accelerator and steer straight until you regain control. Do not use your brakes while hydroplaning, as this may cause total loss of control.

Snow: Treading the Icy Path

Snow-covered roads present a complex challenge, requiring a delicate balance between control and caution. When driving in snowy conditions, remember:

- **Use winter tires:** Put on winter tires or chains for improved traction if possible. Regular tires usually don't provide sufficient traction on icy surfaces.
- **Reduce speed further:** Snowy roads demand even slower speeds. Accelerate, brake, and steer gradually to minimize the risk of skidding.
- **Increase your following distance dramatically:** The stopping distance on snow can be significantly longer. Keep a larger than normal gap between you and the car you are following.
- **Use lower gears:** When descending steep hills, shift to a lower gear to reduce the risk of skidding due to rapid acceleration.

As you drive the varied weather conditions of Florida, remember that adaptation is the key to a safe journey. Embrace the ever-changing elements as opportunities to refine your driving techniques and uphold the responsibility we all share on the road.

ADAPTING TO ROAD CONDITIONS

Each road holds its own narrative and rhythm, demanding your skill and adaptability to ensure your safety and the well-being of other drivers.

The Importance of Road Conditions While Driving

The road is your driving partner, influencing your every turn, stop, and acceleration. Recognizing and adapting to changing road conditions is a skilled and responsible driver trait.

Navigating Uneven Roads: A Smooth Approach

Uneven roads are a frequent companion on your journey, and they demand a measured approach to maintain control and comfort.

- **Reduce speed:** Slow down when encountering uneven surfaces, allowing your vehicle's suspension to absorb the road unevenness and offer a smoother ride.
- **Maintain a steady grip:** Keep a firm but relaxed grip on the steering wheel. Avoid sudden jerks or tight gripping, as these can amplify the impact of bumps.
- **Adjust following distance:** Maintain a slightly greater following distance when driving on uneven roads, giving you extra time to react if your vehicle responds unexpectedly to the road's contours.

Navigating Potholes: Evading the Pitfalls

Potholes can turn an uneventful drive into a challenge, threatening your vehicle's stability and potentially causing damage.

- **Stay alert:** Keep a watchful eye on the road ahead. Potholes can appear suddenly, and your ability to anticipate them is crucial.
- **Reduce speed:** Slow down when approaching areas with pothole potential. Lowering your speed allows you more time to react and make your way around them.
- **Maintain tire pressure:** Properly inflated tires are more resilient to impact. Inspect your tire pressure regularly to lessen the risk of damage.

Navigating Road Construction Areas: A Passage of Caution

Construction zones can disrupt the flow of traffic and present hazards that demand heightened vigilance.

- **Follow signage:** Adhere to posted speed limits and any construction-related signage. Reduced speed limits are often in place to ensure the safety of everyone on the road, including the workers.
- **Merge early:** Follow merge instructions well in advance of lane closures. Last minute lane changes may cause confusion and increase the risk of being involved in a crash.

- **Stay calm and patient:** Road work zones can test your patience, but maintaining a composed attitude contributes to a safer environment for everyone.

As you travel through Florida's diverse landscapes, keep in mind that your ability to adapt is a cornerstone of responsible driving. While road conditions may vary, your dedication to safety and vigilance must remain unwavering.

CITY VS. RURAL DRIVING: NAVIGATING DIVERSE LANDSCAPES

It's important to recognize that the road's character changes as you transition from cityscapes to rural expanses. Each setting presents different challenges that push the driver's skill set to ensure safe navigation.

City Driving: Navigating Urban Labyrinths

Driving in the heart of a bustling city demands a heightened sense of awareness and adaptability.

In city driving, traffic congestion frequently challenges your patience and upends your plans. Negotiating traffic signals, stop signs, and pedestrian crossings requires precise timing and heightened awareness. Keep in mind that urban areas are teeming with pedestrians, cyclists, and motorcyclists. Anticipate unexpected movements from non-motorized road users and proceed with caution at crosswalks.

City driving often requires frequent lane changes and parallel parking. To master these maneuvers, use your mirrors and use turn signals appropriately. Practice smooth lane changes to maintain traffic flow while being attentive to other drivers.

Rural Driving: Embracing Open Spaces

Rural roads offer a departure from the urban frenzy, replacing it with open vistas and unique challenges.

When driving in rural areas, be prepared for the potential of limited services. Gas stations and amenities might be fewer and farther between. Plan your fuel stops and refreshment breaks accordingly to ensure you aren't stranded.

Unpredictable wildlife encounters are another aspect of rural driving. Animals can unexpectedly venture onto rural roads, especially during dawn and dusk. Stay vigilant and reduce your speed if you spot wildlife or notice road signs indicating potential animal crossings.

Rural roads tend to be narrower, so exercise patience and use designated turnouts when necessary to allow faster-moving vehicles to pass safely.

A HERO'S JOURNEY THROUGH THE STORM: A LESSON IN PREPAREDNESS

Real-life stories often emerge as powerful lessons, showcasing the importance of knowledge and preparedness. Let's delve into a heartwarming narrative that exemplifies the impact of prior understanding in tackling challenging driving situations, especially in the face of adverse weather conditions, as provided by Cook (2023).

Meet Jon Gilbert, a seasoned driver who had navigated various roadways for years. One winter's day, a sudden and intense snowstorm descended upon the city, blanketing the streets and highways with treacherous ice. As the city grappled with the sudden freeze, Jon found himself on a perilous journey that would put his driving skills to the ultimate test.

Driving along an icy off-ramp, Jon encountered a scene of chaos. More than 20 vehicles were stranded, their tires slipping and sliding, unable to gain traction on the slippery surface. Traffic had come to a standstill, and the situation seemed dire. However, Jon's years of experience and the wisdom he had accumulated from his driving education courses kicked into action.

As he navigated the icy terrain, he noticed something remarkable. Rather than focusing solely on his journey, he felt a surge of compassion for the stranded drivers around him. He realized he had the skills to help, so he decided to take action.

Jon cautiously approached the off-ramp, drawing from his understanding of safe winter driving. He helped many stranded and freezing people by bringing food and helping them free up their cars that had become stuck in the zone.

Jon assessed the situation, donned his winter gear, and began assisting fellow drivers in need. Armed with his knowledge of how to free stuck vehicles from ice, he used techniques he had learned in his driving education class to help drivers rock their cars gently and strategically to regain traction.

One by one, Jon's efforts bore fruit—he helped free vehicle after vehicle from the icy grip of the off-ramp. His patience, experience, and prior understanding proved invaluable as the hours passed. His actions not only facilitated the flow of traffic but also showcased the power of preparedness in the face of adversity.

Jon's journey that day was more than just a drive through a snowstorm; it was a testament to the impact of responsible driving practices. His story underscores the importance of being equipped with the knowledge to navigate even the most challenging conditions. Through his actions, he demonstrated the power of preparedness. He exemplified the spirit of community and responsibility that defines safe and conscientious driving.

Remember, these practices are the tools that enable you to respond adeptly to real-world situations. By internalizing the principles shared in this chapter, you're well-prepared to navigate the complexities of city and rural driving, handle inclement weather, and embrace the dynamics of freeway travel.

As you move forward, put these ideas into action. The true measure of these practices lies in their implementation on the road. Remember the techniques you've learned here the next time you encounter heavy traffic, a dense fog, or a potholed road. Approach each situation with the confidence and preparedness that come from understanding.

Safe driving practices are just half of the picture. In our next chapter, "Driver Responsibility and Consequences," we'll delve into the legal and social responsibilities you shoulder as a driver and the potential consequences of not following the rules of the road. By understanding the importance of responsible driving behavior, you'll continue to build a foundation of knowledge and behavior that elevates your driving to a higher standard.

So, as you navigate the path ahead, carry the insights of this chapter with you. Let your driving be a testament to your commitment to safety, responsibility, and the well-being of all road users. With every mile you cover, you contribute to a culture of responsible driving, making the road a safer place for everyone.

CHOOSE YOUR OWN DRIVING ADVENTURE

Welcome to the *Choose Your Own Driving Adventure* game, where you get to put your newfound knowledge of best driving practices to the test! As you navigate through different driving scenarios, remember the principles you've learned in this chapter. Select the option that you believe is the best driving practice for each situation. Let's begin!

Scenario 1: City Traffic Challenge

While driving through heavy city traffic, the vehicle ahead of you abruptly comes to a stop. What's the best driving practice?

a) Honk and slam on the brakes.
b) Keep an ample following distance and gently use your brakes.
c) Quickly change lanes to avoid the stopped vehicle.

Scenario 2: Foggy Conditions

You're driving through thick fog where visibility is severely reduced. What's the best driving practice?

a) Turn on your high beams to see better.
b) Increase your speed to pass through the fog faster.
c) Reduce your speed, turn on your low beams, and maintain a safe following distance.

Scenario 3: Rural Road Encounter

While driving on a narrow rural road, you see a group of pedestrians walking along the side. What's the best driving practice?

a) Reduce your speed and provide ample space for the pedestrians by moving over to the opposite lane if it's safe to do so.
b) Slow down and honk your horn to alert the pedestrians of your presence.
c) Continue driving at your current speed. Pedestrians should stay on the sidewalk.

Scenario 4: Icy Road Ahead

You approach a stretch of road covered in ice. What's the best driving practice?

a) Continue driving at your current speed. Your vehicle can handle the ice.

b) Accelerate to get through the icy section more quickly.

c) Lower your speed and maintain a safe distance.

Scenario 5: Freeway Driving

You're on a busy freeway, your exit is 2 miles away and you need to make two lane changes for your exit. What's the best driving practice?

a) Force your way into traffic to make your exit, regardless of the other vehicles.

b) Remain calm, use your turn signal, and make the lane changes one at a time when you find a suitable gap.

c) Slow down and stop if necessary until the other drivers stop as well so you can change lanes.

Scenario 6: Pothole Alert

You spot a deep pothole ahead on the road. What's the best driving practice?

a) Swerve sharply to avoid the pothole, even if it means crossing into another lane.

b) Brace for impact and drive straight over the pothole to minimize vehicle damage.

c) Lower your speed, check your mirrors, and cautiously drive around the pothole.

Your choices reflect your understanding of best driving practices and your commitment to safe and responsible driving. Remember, real-life driving situations may not always have clear-cut options, but your knowledge will guide you in making the right decisions. Keep honing your skills and applying the principles you've learned to ensure a safe and enjoyable driving experience for yourself and others on the road.

Answers:

Scenario 1-b Scenario 2-c Scenario 3-aScenario 4-c Scenario 5-b Scenario 6-c

6

DRIVER RESPONSIBILITY AND CONSEQUENCES

"A dream doesn't become reality through magic; it takes sweat, determination, and hard work."

— COLIN POWELL

As a responsible driver, your obligations go far beyond simply maneuvering a vehicle from point A to point B. Understanding and embracing your responsibilities as a driver is not only a legal requirement but also a moral duty that contributes to the safety and harmony of our roads.

Driving is a privilege that carries a significant weight of responsibility. Beyond the mechanical operation of a vehicle, you're responsible for your safety and the safety of your passengers and others sharing the road. Understanding the rules of the road and adhering to traffic laws are not just legal obligations but also ethical commitments that demonstrate your respect for the lives and well-being of others.

In this chapter, we'll delve into the repercussions of traffic violations, which extend far beyond mere fines. These consequences can have life-altering effects on your driving record, insurance premiums, and personal freedoms. By comprehending the potential aftermath of violating driving rules, you'll be better prepared to prioritize safety and compliance.

Insurance plays a critical role in the realm of driving responsibilities. We'll discuss the various types of coverage available to drivers and underscore the importance of maintaining adequate protection. Understanding how insurance functions and its role in alleviating financial burdens resulting from accidents is essential for being a responsible driver.

The goal of this chapter is to cultivate a sense of responsibility among drivers. A knowledgeable driver can make decisions that enhance their safety and that of others. Understanding the wide-ranging effects of driving actions enables us to collectively promote a culture of safety, courtesy, and adherence to the law on the roads.

By the end of this chapter, you'll have a thorough understanding of the multifaceted responsibilities that come with driving. We'll explore the potential repercussions of neglecting these responsibilities, aiming to give you a clear grasp of both the legal and ethical obligations that accompany driving privileges.

So, let's delve into driver responsibility and consequences as we equip you with the knowledge and insights necessary for a lifetime of responsible and mindful driving.

LEGAL AND MORAL RESPONSIBILITIES

Legal Obligations

Driving a vehicle isn't solely about steering, accelerating, and braking. It entails a set of legal obligations that all drivers must follow to ensure the safety and order of our roads. These obligations are in place not only to protect you but also to safeguard the lives of those sharing the road with you.

- **Adhering to traffic laws:** Being a responsible driver entails having a thorough understanding of Florida's traffic laws, which include following speed limits, obeying traffic signs and signals, yielding the right-of-way, and making complete stops at stop signs and red lights. Disregarding these laws not only exposes you to legal consequences but also endangers the safety of all road users.
- **Driving sober:** One of the most crucial legal responsibilities is to drive sober. It is unlawful to operate a vehicle under the influence of drugs or alcohol because it jeopardizes your safety and that of others on the road. Driving impaired severely impairs judgment, reflexes, and decision-making, significantly raising accident risks with catastrophic consequences.
- **Maintaining a valid driver's license:** Acquiring a driver's license is both a privilege and a legal necessity to operate a vehicle. It indicates that you have fulfilled the required criteria and proven your capability to drive safely. It's crucial to renew your license on time and adhere to any restrictions or endorsements specified on it.

Moral Responsibilities

In addition to legal obligations, being a driver also entails moral responsibilities. These responsibilities align with both the law and your ethical duty to foster a safe and harmonious driving environment.

- **Respecting other drivers' safety:** Every driver on the road is entitled to a safe journey. This means drivers should not engage in aggressive or reckless behaviors that could endanger their lives; instead, they should follow behaviors that promote safety, such as maintaining a safe following distance, using turn signals appropriately, and refraining from distractions while driving.
- **Making ethical decisions on the road:** The road is full of unexpected situations that require split-second decisions. Ethical driving means prioritizing others' safety over personal convenience. This includes yielding to pedestrians, giving way to emergency vehicles, and driving carefully in bad weather. Remember, everyone's actions impact road safety.

It's imperative to know that being a responsible driver means following the law and prioritizing the safety of others. This creates a safer and more cooperative driving environment for everyone.

DRIVING WITHOUT A LICENSE

Understanding that having a driver's license is a privilege makes it vital to discuss the ramifications of driving without a valid driver's license. The Florida Vehicle Code addresses the offense of failing to show a driver's license when operating a motor vehicle. This section underscores the significance of always carrying a valid driver's license while driving.

Individuals operating a motor vehicle are required to have their driver's license with them and must be able to present it to a law enforcement officer upon their request; this is essential for verifying that drivers are authorized to operate a vehicle and have met the necessary qualifications.

Failure to present a valid driver's license can result in various legal consequences. It's imperative to understand that these consequences are in place to encourage responsible and compliant behavior among drivers.

- **Legal penalties:** If you cannot present a valid driver's license upon request by a law enforcement officer, you may face legal penalties. These penalties could include fines, which may vary depending on the circumstances, including any prior violations.
- **Impact on driving record:** Violations in this section can result in points added to your driving record. Accumulating points on your record can lead to higher insurance rates and a potential driver's license suspension.
- **Compromised insurance:** Driving without a valid driver's license can impact your insurance coverage. In the event of an accident, car insurance companies may use your lack of a valid driver's license as grounds to deny coverage, leaving you personally responsible for any resulting damages or liabilities.

Driving without a driver's license is an infraction. Be sure to follow this regulation to avoid legal consequences and contribute to our roads' overall safety and accountability.

ALCOHOL AND DRUGS: ETHICAL DECISION MAKING BEHIND THE WHEEL—A DRIVING SIMULATOR STUDY

Alcohol and drugs are substances that can significantly impair a driver's abilities, leading to compromised judgment, coordination, and reaction times. It's crucial to acknowledge that operating a vehicle while under the influence is not only a legal violation but also an irresponsible action that jeopardizes the safety of oneself and others on the road.

The Driving Simulator Study: Ethical Decision-Making

The driving simulator study discussed in this chapter aimed to explore how drivers make ethical decisions when confronted with situations involving alcohol or drugs. This study placed participants in various simulated scenarios, assessing their choices when presented with opportunities to avoid driving under the influence (Samuel, et. al., 2020).

Study Outcomes: Ethical Dilemmas and Responsible Choices

The driving simulator study yielded important insights into the ethical dilemmas drivers encounter and the decisions they make under the influence of substances. Some outcomes included

- **Impaired judgment:** Participants who consumed alcohol or drugs in the simulated scenarios exhibited poor judgment, leading them to underestimate the risks of driving under the influence.
- **Increased risk-taking:** The study revealed that under the influence, participants were more likely to engage in risky behaviors such as speeding, weaving between lanes, and failing to obey traffic signals.

- **Inhibited reaction times:** Driving simulator data indicated that alcohol and drugs hindered participants' ability to react promptly to unexpected events on the road.
- **Ethical decision-making:** Despite the impairments caused by substances, some participants exhibited responsible, ethical decision-making by opting not to drive and seeking alternative modes of transportation.

IMPLICATIONS FOR RESPONSIBLE DRIVING

The driving simulator study highlights the vital need for responsible decision-making regarding alcohol and drugs. It emphasizes that driving under the influence poses a serious threat to lives and reflects an ethical lapse.

As responsible drivers, we must heed the study's findings, prioritize safety, and avoid driving after consuming alcohol or drugs. Seeking alternative options like designated drivers or rideshare services is crucial. Making ethical choices ensures a safer driving environment and upholds our responsibilities as licensed drivers.

Consequences of Violations: Florida Traffic Ticket Fines and Penalties

The traffic citation fines serve as a deterrent for rule violations and promote responsible driving behavior. Fines vary based on the nature of the offense, the severity of the violation, and any prior infractions. It's vital to recognize that fines are not just financial consequences but also serve to make drivers reconsider their actions and encourage adherence to the law.

Traffic offenses, in addition to fines, accumulate points on your driving history. These points serve as a measure of your driving behavior and can have significant consequences:

- **Insurance rates:** An increased tally of points on your driving record can result in higher insurance rates. Insurance companies view drivers with points as higher-risk clients, resulting in higher costs for coverage.
- **Driver's license suspension:** Accumulating too many infraction points within a specific time frame (12 points in a 12-month period is a 30-day suspension, 18 points in an 18-month period is a 180-day suspension, 24 points in a 36-month period is a 1 year suspension) can lead to your driver's license being suspended. Certain violations carry more severe penalties, such as license suspension or even revocation. Suspension means the loss of driving privileges for a designated amount of time. If your driver's license is revoked, it means permanent termination of your driver's license.

Understanding the Gravity

It's essential to recognize that traffic rule violations aren't mere inconveniences—they carry real and impactful consequences. Responsible driving is not only about avoiding fines but also about prioritizing safety, respecting the law, and contributing to the well-being of everyone on the road.

Fines, points, license suspension, and even imprisonment underscore the gravity of adhering to traffic laws. Being aware of the potential repercussions allows you to make choices that prioritize safety and responsible driving.

Remember that every decision you make on the road has implications beyond the immediate moment. You play a significant role in creating a safer and more cooperative driving environment for all road users by upholding your driving responsibilities.

ROLE OF INSURANCE

Having car insurance is a legal requirement to drive in the state of Florida. It is a safety net that safeguards you, your passengers, and other road users from the financial and legal consequences of accidents. Adequate insurance coverage is essential to responsible driving, ensuring you're prepared for unforeseen circumstances and capable of fulfilling your obligations in case of accidents or injuries. Florida has the No-Fault Law: All drivers are to carry a minimum of $10,000 in Personal Injury Protection (PIP) and $10,000 in Property Damage Liability (PDL).

Different Types of Coverage

Understanding the various insurance coverage options is vital for making informed decisions about which policy to choose:

- **Personal Injury Protection (PIP):** Provides coverage for injuries in a collision regardless of fault.
- **Property Damage Liability (PDL):** Provides coverage for property that you damage.
- **Uninsured/Underinsured motorist coverage:** This type of auto insurance offers coverage in the event of an accident caused by an underinsured or uninsured driver.

Driving Without Insurance: Consequences for Driving Without Insurance in Florida

Florida law mandates that all drivers have at least the minimum required vehicle insurance coverage. Each driver needs to evaluate their unique financial situation, including net worth, to ensure they are insured adequately, protecting themselves and others on the road from the financial burdens arising from accidents and unforeseen circumstances.

Penalties for Driving Without Insurance

Driving without the minimum required insurance coverage in Florida carries a range of penalties designed to encourage compliance with the law and promote responsible driving behavior. Driving without the required insurance coverage in Florida results in penalties aimed at enforcing compliance and responsible driving. This includes fines and potential license suspension, which can alter your way of life.

In certain circumstances, law enforcement may impound your vehicle if you're caught driving without insurance. This impoundment can result in additional expenses and inconvenience. If you're involved in an accident without insurance, you could be personally liable for covering the costs of physical damages, medical expenses, and legal fees for both your vehicle and the other party involved.

Impact on Future Insurance Rates

In addition to the immediate penalties, driving without insurance can impact your future insurance rates. Suppose you're able to obtain insurance after the violation. In that case, your premiums will likely increase significantly due to the higher perceived risk associated with your driving history.

The Responsible Choice

Driving without insurance violates the law and exposes you to substantial financial risks and potential legal consequences. It's essential to recognize that having insurance coverage is not just a legal requirement—it's a responsible decision that reflects your commitment to accountability on the road.

ADDITIONAL TYPES OF CAR INSURANCE AVAILABLE IN FLORIDA

A solid understanding of these insurance options is essential for every responsible driver. Each type of coverage serves a specific purpose, contributing to your safety and financial security on the road. Let's explore the six types available in Florida, according to the DMV (n.d.).

Bodily Injury Liability (BI)

Pays for death or serious and permanent injury to others when you are at fault. This coverage helps protect you financially if you're at fault in an accident that injures others as well as assisting in covering any legal fees.

Comprehensive Coverage

This type of insurance safeguards your vehicle against non-collision incidents such as theft, vandalism, natural disasters, and animal collisions. It offers financial assistance to repair or replace your vehicle in these scenarios.

Collision Coverage

This type of insurance policy provides coverage when your vehicle gets damaged in a collision, regardless of who's at fault. This coverage assists in covering the repair or replacement of your car in case it sustains damage in a collision.

Uninsured/Underinsured Motorist Coverage

Uninsured/Underinsured Motorist coverage is essential as it provides protection in the event of a collision caused by a driver with no insurance or insufficient coverage to fully compensate for your injuries and damages. This coverage ensures you're not left bearing the financial burden due to the other person's lack of or insufficient insurance.

Medical Payments Coverage (Med Pay)

This type of policy includes coverage for medical expenses resulting from a car accident, regardless of fault. It encompasses hospital bills, doctor visits, and other medical costs for both you and your passengers.

Gap Coverage

Gap Coverage is relevant if you have a leased or financed vehicle. In the event of a total loss (when your car is considered a write-off due to a severe accident), Gap Coverage helps cover any difference between the loan balance and the value of your vehicle, preventing you from being financially responsible with the lien holder for the difference.

CHOOSING THE RIGHT COVERAGE

Selecting the appropriate types and amount of insurance coverage is critical to responsible driving. Your coverage should align with your needs, financial situation, and driving habits. Understanding the various types of coverage empowers you to make informed decisions prioritizing your safety, security, and compliance with the law.

REAL-LIFE ANECDOTE: CONSEQUENCES OF IRRESPONSIBILITY ON THE ROAD

In exploring driver responsibility and consequences, it's crucial to understand the real-life impact of irresponsibility behind the wheel. The story of State Representative Dan Wolgamott serves as a stark reminder of the severe repercussions that can arise from poor decision-making on the road (Faircloth, 2023).

In a recent incident, Representative Dan Wolgamott faced the consequences of a DWI (Driving While Intoxicated) arrest. This event serves as an illustration of the severe legal and personal ramifications that can result from driving under the influence.

Upon reflection, Representative Wolgamott publicly acknowledged his error and took full responsibility for his actions. His story underscores the importance of accountability and the recognition that even individuals in positions of authority are not exempt from the consequences of irresponsible behavior on the road.

Driving under the influence endangers the driver's life and threatens other road users and pedestrians. The incident is a stark reminder that adherence to traffic laws, responsible decision-making, and prioritizing the safety of oneself and others are fundamental aspects of being a responsible driver.

This story serves as a cautionary tale that resonates with all drivers. It emphasizes the need to recognize the gravity of poor choices on the road and the subsequent impact on one's life, reputation, and legal standing. By learning from real-life anecdotes like this, we gain valuable insights into the consequences of irresponsibility, promoting a culture of accountability, safety, and responsibility among drivers.

As we progress in our journey of becoming informed and responsible drivers, let's keep in mind that defensive driving techniques play a role in preventing accidents and violations. In the upcoming chapter, "Mastering Defensive Driving Techniques," we will delve into these strategies that empower you to anticipate, respond, and adapt to the unpredictable nature of the road.

Remember, responsible driving isn't just about following the rules—it's about embodying a mindset prioritizing safety, respect, and accountability.

INTERACTIVE QUIZ: TESTING YOUR UNDERSTANDING OF DRIVER RESPONSIBILITY AND CONSEQUENCES

Let's put your knowledge of driver responsibility and consequences to the test with some scenario-based questions. Consider each situation carefully and select the response that you believe reflects the responsible and safe course of action.

Scenario 1

Being a responsible driver means you have _____ obligations:

    a) Moral.
    b) Legal.
    c) Both of the above.

Scenario 2

Points on your driving record can lead to license suspension, the following will cause a suspension:

    a) 8 or more points in one year
    b) 12 or more points in one year.
    c) 10 or more points in one year.

Scenario 3

The minimum auto insurance requirements in Florida are:

    a) $10,000 Personal Injury Protection (PIP) and $10,000 Property Damage Liability (PDL).
    b) $20,000 Personal Injury Protection (PIP) and $20,000 Property Damage Liability (PDL).
    c) $15,000 Personal Injury Protection (PIP) and $5,000 Property Damage Liability (PDL).

Scenario 4

You're at a party and have had a couple of alcoholic drinks. Your friends are recommending that you drive home. What is the responsible decision?

    a) Accept their offer and drive home carefully.
    b) Wait a bit longer and have a few more drinks before driving.

c) Politely decline and arrange for a sober driver, taxi, or rideshare.

Scenario 5

To choose the correct auto insurance for you, it is vital to consider:

a) Your net worth.
b) If driving with the minimum required limits leaves you financially exposed.
c) Both a and b.

Scenario 6

Driving without auto insurance:

a) Is allowed as long as you are driving by yourself and avoid congested roads.
b) Is against the law.
c) Is allowed as long as it was vital to not get in trouble at your job.

Your responses demonstrate your understanding of responsible driving practices and their potential consequences. Remember that responsible driving isn't just about following rules; it's about prioritizing safety, making ethical choices, and contributing to a secure and cooperative driving environment. Keep up the good work as you continue your journey to becoming a knowledgeable and responsible driver.

Answers

Scenario 1-c Scenario 2-b Scenario 3-a Scenario 4-c Scenario 5-c
Scenario 6-b

7

MASTERING DEFENSIVE DRIVING TECHNIQUES

"An ounce of prevention is worth a pound of cure."

— BENJAMIN FRANKLIN

In this case, defensive driving is that "ounce of prevention" when you're behind the wheel, potentially saving lives.

Defensive driving isn't just another phase of operating a vehicle—it's a mindset, a way of perceiving the road that empowers you to anticipate, adapt, and react adeptly to potential hazards. It goes beyond basic traffic rules and maneuvers; it's about being prepared for the unexpected and safeguarding yourself, your passengers, and other road users from harm.

Throughout this chapter, we'll explore a range of defensive driving techniques that will sharpen your instincts, enhance your situational awareness, and equip you to navigate even the trickiest of road scenarios confidently. From maintaining a safe following distance to recognizing and responding to aggressive driving behaviors, each technique you learn here will contribute to a comprehensive toolkit that can be the difference between an uneventful journey and a regrettable mishap.

But why is mastering defensive driving so crucial? It extends beyond obeying traffic laws; it involves taking personal responsibility for your actions on the road. By integrating these techniques into your driving habits, you safeguard yourself and other drivers, promoting a safer driving atmosphere for everyone. This proactive approach decreases the risk of accidents, mitigates injuries, and even aids in easing traffic congestion, leading to smoother and more efficient everyday commutes. Let's delve into the nuances of defensive driving and equip you to tackle road challenges with expertise and confidence.

EXPLANATION OF DEFENSIVE DRIVING

As responsible drivers, we perceive that the road is an ever-changing environment, and potential dangers can arise at any moment. The concept of defensive driving revolves around minimizing risks and ensuring the safety of all road users through a combination of prudent actions and a heightened understanding of road dynamics.

A vital piece of defensive driving is anticipation. It entails surveying the road ahead to spot potential hazards in advance, providing you with sufficient time to respond appropriately. By keeping your attention ahead, you'll notice approaching intersections, pedestrians, and vehicles entering the road. Anticipating the behavior of other drivers enables you to adapt your speed and position, averting potential conflicts. Keep in mind that the more time you have to react, the greater your likelihood of avoiding an accident.

Awareness is the foundation of defensive driving, requiring constant vigilance of your surroundings. This entails monitoring the road ahead, as well as regularly checking mirrors and blind spots. By maintaining comprehensive awareness, you can identify potential risks from all directions, enabling quick decision-making when necessary. Achieving this skill involves minimizing distractions in the vehicle and remaining attuned to changing road conditions.

Then, preparation is key to defensive driving, involving strategic vehicle positioning for visibility and minimizing blind spots. Maintain ample following distance for quick braking or maneuvering, and keep hands on the wheel and foot near the brake pedal for instant responses to unforeseen circumstances.

The essence of defensive is demonstrated by reacting calmly and effectively to various road situations, from sudden lane changes to emergencies and adverse weather. Prioritize safety, signal early, and communicate clearly with other drivers. By embracing these principles, you take control of your driving environment, enhancing safety for all, regardless of right-of-way.

THE KEYS TO DEFENSIVE DRIVING AND COLLISION AVOIDANCE

In our pursuit of mastering defensive driving techniques, we must equip ourselves with essential keys that unlock the door to safe, responsible, and proactive driving. These keys encapsulate the core principles that underscore the philosophy of defensive driving and serve as your guiding beacons on the road.

Think Safety First

Safety is more than just a priority; it's a way of thinking. Every decision you make behind the wheel should be rooted in the concern for your safety and the safety of others, adhering to traffic rules, restraining from risky maneuvers, and prioritizing caution over haste.

Be Aware of Your Surroundings—Pay Attention

Awareness is your sentinel against potential hazards. Stay vigilant on the road by scanning ahead, checking mirrors, and monitoring the movement of surrounding vehicles. This acute awareness helps you identify potential threats early, providing ample time and space for a proper response. Your attentiveness is key to maintaining a strong defensive driving posture.

Do Not Depend on Other Drivers

Defensive driving rests on self-reliance. Anticipate but don't depend solely on others. Keep a safe distance, signal clearly, and be ready for surprises. Taking charge of your safety ensures you can react to unexpected moves.

Follow the Recommended Following Distance

Always maintain the recommended following distance of four seconds. To check if you're following this distance, pick a fixed point on the road ahead and time how long it takes for your vehicle to reach it after the one in front passes. This gap allows you enough time to react to sudden stops or slowdowns. In adverse weather like rain or low visibility, increase this distance for added safety.

Keep Your Speed Down

Speed directly impacts your reaction time and the severity of accidents. Adhering to speed limits is a legal requirement, but more importantly, adjust your speed to match road conditions. Driving within a safe speed range enhances your ability to perceive and react to potential dangers.

Have an Escape Route

Continuously think of an escape route. Visualize open spaces, shoulders, or adjacent lanes you can move into if a sudden hazard arises. This mental preparedness ensures that you're never boxed in and have room to maneuver away from potential collisions.

Separate Risks

Reduce risk by maintaining space around your vehicle. Avoid driving alongside other vehicles for extended periods, as you might be in the other driver's blind spot. Whenever possible, maintain a buffer zone on all sides, reducing the chance of a collision if another driver makes an unexpected move.

Cut Out Distractions

Stay focused on the road to maintain your defensive driving stance. Refrain from using your phone, adjusting the radio, or participating in activities that divert your attention from driving. By eliminating distractions, you enhance your ability to anticipate and respond to potential hazards, ensuring safer driving conditions.

HANDLING DANGEROUS SITUATIONS

It's essential to acknowledge that the road isn't always a predictable and serene environment. There are times when unexpected obstacles and difficult situations arise. You must remain calm to make split-second decisions, which is the difference between avoiding a collision or making it a minor collision rather than a major one if the crash is unavoidable.

On-Road Obstacles

Scenario: You're driving along an unfamiliar route, and there are high gusts of wind. Suddenly, a large tree branch falls onto the road.

- **Step 1:** Maintain a safe following distance greater than four seconds due to the high wind; this gives you ample time to react to unforeseen obstacles.
- **Step 2:** Keep scanning ahead, noting potential hazards like debris, animals, or stalled vehicles.

- **Step 3:** When confronted with this obstacle, resist the urge to swerve abruptly. Instead, brake smoothly and steer around gradually without losing control.

These techniques prepare you to navigate unexpected obstacles without jeopardizing your safety or the safety of others.

Navigating Aggressive Drivers

One of the most challenging scenarios you may encounter is interacting with aggressive drivers. These individuals can turn a routine commute into a tense situation, testing your patience and skills.

Deal With Patience

- **Step 1:** Stay calm and composed. Do not allow another driver's aggression to affect your emotional state.
- **Step 2:** Avoid aggressive gestures, shouting matches, or retaliating. These behaviors only escalate the situation.

Patience and calmness are your allies in diffusing tense situations and upholding the principles of defensive driving.

Drive Defensively

- **Step 1:** Focus on your driving but stay vigilant by scanning. Keep a safe following distance and obey traffic rules.
- **Step 2:** Avoid any behavior that might provoke or worsen the situation. Maintain a steady speed and predictable movements.

Defensive driving involves prioritizing safety and responsibility, regardless of the behavior of other drivers.

Fighting Back and Overcoming Emotional Distress

- **Step 1:** Refrain from taking the actions of aggressive drivers personally. Their behavior often stems from unrelated factors.
- **Step 2:** Focus on your well-being and safety, as your goal is to arrive at your destination safely.

Overcoming emotional distress empowers you to stay in control and make rational decisions on the road.

Politely Deal With Other Drivers

- **Step 1:** If confronted by another driver, avoid making eye contact or engaging in arguments.
- **Step 2:** If another driver attempts to engage you, remain polite but noncommittal. Do not engage in verbal disputes.
- **Step 3:** If the other driver continues to be a threat, dial 911 to get assistance from law enforcement and drive to the nearest police station or a public place, reducing the chances of the situation escalating further.

Maintaining your composure and civility prevents the situation from escalating and ensures your safety.

Maintain a Distance

- **Step 1:** Keep a safe following distance from aggressive drivers, allowing you space to react to their sudden maneuvers.
- **Step 2:** If an aggressive driver tailgates you, maintain your speed and avoid speeding up to appease them.

Maintaining a safe distance is crucial in avoiding collisions and preventing the aggressive behavior of others from affecting your driving.

DEALING WITH AGGRESSIVE DRIVERS: SCENARIOS

Scenario 1: An Impatient Driver Behind You is Tailgating and Honking Incessantly.

- **Step 1:** Avoid engaging in aggressive behavior or retaliating. Stay focused on your driving.
- **Step 2:** Keep a steady speed and signal your intention to change lanes.

In this case, you retain control over the situation, ensuring your safety and that of other road users.

Scenario 2: Another Driver Reacts Aggressively to a Driving Error You've Made, Escalating the Situation Into a Road Rage Incident.

- **Step 1:** It's best to avoid eye contact or interacting with an irate driver. Concentrate on safe and responsible driving.
- **Step 2:** If the situation worsens, call law enforcement or drive to a public area if you feel threatened.
- **Step 3:** Do not let road rage affect your emotions or driving behavior. Stay composed and adhere to the principles of defensive driving.

This approach helps you control your reactions, mitigating potential risks associated with road rage incidents.

Navigating aggressive drivers requires a delicate balance of patience, composure, and defensive driving skills. Employing these strategies provides you with the best opportunity to prevent a road rage incident.

BENEFITS OF DEFENSIVE DRIVING

The advantages extend far beyond merely passing your DMV exam. Embracing defensive driving principles can significantly enhance your driving experience, making you a safer, more responsible and confident driver.

Improves Your Driving Skills

Mastering defensive driving techniques sharpens your driving skills across the board. You become more attuned to road conditions, traffic patterns, and the behavior of other drivers; this heightened awareness translates to improved control over your vehicle, smoother maneuvering, and enhanced decision-making skills while on the road.

Accident-Free Techniques

The core philosophy of defensive driving revolves around minimizing risks and preventing accidents by implementing proactive safety measures. By maintaining safe following distances, scanning the road ahead, and obeying traffic rules, you enhance your protection in unforeseen situations, reducing the chances of collisions and near misses.

No Violation Charges

Defensive driving techniques align with traffic laws and regulations; driving defensively minimizes the chances of receiving traffic citations, thus keeping your driving record clean and ensuring your auto insurance rates stay as low as possible.

Less Maintenance

Defensive driving practices extend the lifespan of your vehicle. You reduce wear and tear on your vehicle's components by avoiding sudden stops, maintaining a safe distance, and driving smoothly. The result is fewer repairs, which saves you money and a longer-lasting vehicle.

Mitigating Traffic Congestion

Defensive driving isn't just about reacting to immediate dangers; it's about preventing the domino effect of accidents that can cascade into massive traffic congestion. By practicing anticipatory and cautious driving, you contribute to the uninterrupted flow of traffic, minimizing delays and ensuring that the roadways remain efficient.

Reducing Economic Impact

Accidents don't just take a physical and emotional toll—they also carry a significant economic burden. Defensive driving mitigates this impact by reducing the occurrence of accidents and their subsequent costs, including medical expenses, property damage, and increased auto insurance rates.

Enhancing Personal Confidence

By internalizing the principles of anticipation, awareness, and preparedness, you've embraced a proactive approach to driving—one that prioritizes safety, responsibility, and respect for fellow road users. You've discovered how maintaining a safe following distance, scanning the road, adapting to weather conditions, and respecting other drivers can all contribute to a safer driving experience.

As you move forward, keep in mind that defensive driving is a mindset, not just a set of techniques. By incorporating these principles into your driving habits, you're not only protecting yourself but also enhancing road safety for everyone. Your journey towards responsible, proactive, and skilled driving is underway, with the next chapter bringing you closer to success on the road and in the DMV exam.

DECISION-MAKING GAME

With a decision-making game, let's test your newfound knowledge of defensive driving techniques. This game will present you with a series of road scenarios, each with multiple choices. Your task is to choose the response that best aligns with the principles of defensive driving.

Scenario 1: Erratically Driving Vehicle

You're driving on a busy highway, and a car ahead of you is driving erratically. What's the best defensive driving response?

a) Increase the following distance and stay behind the erratically driving car.
b) Brake suddenly to assure you stay as far as possible.
c) Increase your speed to pass the car driving erratically; it's safer to be in front.

Scenario 2: Actively Scan While You Drive

While driving through a residential area, a child suddenly runs out onto the road chasing a ball. What's the best defensive driving response?

a) Honk loudly and continue driving at your current speed.
b) Immediately swerve sharply to avoid hitting the child.
c) Brake as gently as possible while still assuring you do not hit the child, come to a controlled stop, and honk to alert the child.

Scenario 3: Unpredictable Merge

You're on the rightmost lane on a freeway, and the driver in the merging lane seems unaware of your presence. What's the best defensive driving response?

a) Speed up to stay ahead of them and assert your position.
b) If it is safe, change lanes or adjust your speed accordingly to allow room for the other driver to merge without colliding with you.
c) Maintain your speed and force them to yield to you.

Scenario 4: Unpredictable Hazard

You're driving on a busy city street, and the car in front of you suddenly slams on its brakes for an object on the road. What's the best defensive driving response?

a) Swerve into the next lane at once to avoid rear-ending the car.
b) Honk loudly to express your frustration with the sudden stop.
c) Keep an adequate following distance and brake smoothly to come to a controlled stop.

Scenario 5: Blind Intersection

You are at a one-way stop, and overgrown bushes obstruct your view; you can't see if any vehicles are coming from the side street. What's the best defensive driving response?

a) Quickly accelerate to cross the intersection before any cars approach.
b) Stop behind the limit line, then inch forward slowly until you get a view past the bushes and proceed once you confirm it is safe to do so.

c) Stop a few feet past the stop line to get a better view of the side street.

Scenario 6: Honking From Another Driver

While attempting to merge onto a highway, another driver honks angrily at you for trying to merge at a slower speed. What's the best defensive driving response?

a) Adjust your speed accordingly for your safety and that of the other driver and determine if it is safer to merge behind the other driver instead of trying to merge ahead.
b) Ignore them and continue merging at your own pace.
c) Use your brakes abruptly to teach them a valuable lesson.

Scenario 7: Tailgating Challenge

You notice a car tailgating closely behind you, even though you're already driving at the speed limit. What's the best defensive driving response?

a) Tap your brakes to warn them about their following distance.
b) Do a sudden slow-down.
c) When safe, make a lane change.

Remember, your choices on the road are essential in ensuring the safety of yourself and others. As you progress in your journey, reflect on the scenarios and responses provided. Let your commitment to defensive driving guide your actions in real-world situations.

Answers
Scenario 1: a) Scenario 2: c) Scenario 3: b) Scenario 4: c)
Scenario 5: b) Scenario 6: a) Scenario 7: c)

8

HELPFUL RESOURCES

"An investment in knowledge pays the best interest."

— BENJAMIN FRANKLIN

Congratulations on making your way through our *Florida DMV Exam Handbook*! By now, you've absorbed a wealth of knowledge about the rules of the road, defensive driving practices, and the responsibilities of obtaining a learner's permit. But your learning journey doesn't end with the test: It marks the beginning of a lifelong dedication to safe and conscientious driving practices.

In this section, you'll find a curated list of resources, including materials, websites, and organizations, offering extensive information on driving, traffic regulations, and road safety. Whether you're a new driver building confidence or a seasoned one staying updated with Florida's driving laws, these resources are invaluable.

So, as you reach the end of this handbook, keep in mind that becoming a skilled driver is an ongoing process. The resources provided here will be your guides, helping you navigate towards a safer and more confident driving experience. Embrace them, learn from them, and drive responsibly to protect yourself and others. Safe driving is not just a skill—it's a commitment that starts with knowledge and resources at your disposal.

WEBSITES, APPS, AND BOOKS

In your journey to becoming an informed driver in Florida, it's crucial to harness the power of various resources beyond the confines of this handbook. These include official websites, mobile apps, and official vehicle code books to enhance your understanding of road rules, driving laws, and safety practices. Additionally, we'll discuss the potential benefits of utilizing local library resources.

DMV Florida (Official Website)

https://www.flhsmv.gov/

The Florida Department of Motor Vehicles (DMV) maintains an official website that serves as a treasure trove of information. Here, you'll find comprehensive details on driver's licensing, vehicle registration, traffic laws, and anything related to vehicle matters, and is an excellent resource for exam preparation.

Driving-Tests.org & dmv-written-test.com/Florida

https://driving-tests.org/

https://www.dmv-written-test.com/Florida/practice-test-1.html

Driving-Tests.org and dmv-written-test.com are valuable platforms offering a collection of practice exams tailored to Florida's DMV requirements. Their user-friendly app is designed to help you prepare thoroughly for the DMV written test. You can access a variety of practice questions and simulations to boost your confidence.

Driving Books

Several reputable books are dedicated to safe driving practices and preparing for the DMV exam, like the *Florida Driver Handbook* (the official DMV handbook), which provides comprehensive insights into Florida's driving laws, road signs, and safe driving tips. It can serve as valuable reference material as you embark on your journey to becoming a responsible driver.

To ensure that you derive the maximum benefit from these resources, it's important to approach your learning journey with a structured and proactive mindset.

UTILIZING RESOURCES

To ensure you benefit from these resources, approach your learning journey with a structured and proactive mindset.

Subscribe to Newsletters

Stay informed about changes in Florida driving laws and regulations by subscribing to newsletters from trusted sources. The DMV's official website often provides updates and newsletters to help you stay current.

Participate in Online Forums

Engage with the driving community by joining online forums or discussion boards dedicated to driving in Florida. These platforms can be valuable for asking questions, sharing experiences, and learning from other drivers.

Stay Up to Date

Driving laws and regulations may change over time. Make it a habit to check for updates on the DMV's website and other trusted sources. Keeping your knowledge current is essential, even after passing your initial exam.

Seek Guidance When Needed

Feel free to seek advice from a driving instructor, mentor, or experienced driver if you encounter challenging concepts or have questions. Getting clarification on doubts can prevent misunderstandings down the road.

Stay Committed to Safe Driving

Remember that the ultimate goal of all this learning is to become a safe and responsible driver. Apply what you've learned not just during your exam but in your everyday driving experiences.

These resources are invaluable tools, and by using them effectively, you'll not only pass the test but also become a more knowledgeable and confident driver on Florida's roads.

Obtaining Your Driver's License

Congratulations! You have now attained your learner's permit, allowing you to practice driving, but one crucial step remains the driving test. You must return to the DMV to take the practical driving test. For minors, there is a 1 year wait period before being eligible to take the behind-the-wheel test. During this examination, the examiner will assess these driving skills to ensure you can safely navigate Florida's roads. Stop signs, traffic signals, intersection observance, turns, right-of-way, backing, quick stop and parallel parking. Upon passing the driving test, you will receive a full-fledged driver's license from the DMV.

Updating Your Insurance

With the attainment of your driver's license, it's essential to consider your financial responsibility as a driver. Florida requires all drivers to have auto insurance coverage. It's your responsibility to obtain an insurance policy that meets the minimum requirements set by the state. Contact local insurance providers to obtain the necessary coverage and ensure you comply with Florida's insurance laws.

Vehicle Registration Requirements

Additionally, as a vehicle owner in Florida, you'll need to ensure that your vehicle's registration is current. Registering your vehicle involves providing the DMV with essential information, such as its year, make, and vehicle identification number (VIN). After the initial vehicle registration, there will be annual renewal fees and annual vehicle inspections.

For a detailed guide on vehicle registration requirements and how to complete the process, consider referring to the official DMV resources or seeking assistance from your local DMV office.

In-Car Driving Lessons

Although professional driving lessons are not required, they are highly recommended for your overall safety and to be ready to demonstrate complete vehicle control to pass the behind-the-wheel test. Keep in mind that the learner's permit is only valid for driving when accompanied by a licensed driver aged 21 or older. Additionally, all minors are required to complete 50 hours of practice, including a minimum of 10 hours during nighttime.

SAFE DRIVING POST-LICENSE: A LIFELONG COMMITMENT TO RESPONSIBLE DRIVING

It's important to know that the road to becoming a safe driver doesn't conclude with the issuance of your license; it is an enduring commitment. In this section, we will emphasize the critical importance of continuing safe driving habits, including defensive driving, abstaining from alcohol while driving, and adhering to speed limits.

Defensive Driving

Remember that adopting a defensive driving mindset is one of the fundamental principles of safe driving. This approach means staying alert and prepared for the unexpected on the road. Defensive drivers anticipate possible hazards, keep a safe following distance, and stay watchful of the behaviors of other road users.

Say No to Drinking and Driving

It should go without saying, but we must emphasize the importance of never getting behind the wheel after consuming alcohol. Driving under the influence poses an enormous risk to your safety and others on the road. Always assign a designated driver or utilize alternative transportation if you've consumed alcohol. The consequences of driving under the influence are both legally and morally severe.

Respect Speed Limits

Speed limits are not random figures; they are established to guarantee safe travel on the road. Excessive speed diminishes reaction time and augments the severity of accidents. It is crucial to consistently abide by posted speed limits, particularly in inclement weather or regions with substantial pedestrian traffic.

Benefits of Safe Driving Rewards

Safe driving not only prevents accidents but also leads to financial benefits. Maintaining a clean driving record and practicing responsible habits can lower insurance premiums and reduce the likelihood of fines or savings.

Passing the written exam is just the beginning of your journey as a licensed driver in Florida. Remember to schedule your driving test, obtain auto insurance, and ensure proper vehicle registration. Embrace the responsibility of safe driving, consider additional training, and prioritize safety.

As we conclude this chapter, we encourage you to put the ideas presented here into action.

Don't forget driving is a privilege and responsibility that affects safety. With the knowledge and resources you have, you're prepared to drive confidently and responsibly. Safe travels on your journey as a responsible driver.

DISCLAIMER

As we begin the practice exams, it is essential to understand that it would be virtually impossible for this book to cover every possible scenario or Florida driving law you might encounter in the DMV knowledge test. Additionally we would like to remind you to please not go directly to the practice exams without reading the material in the book. The questions can vary in wording significantly on the exam, therefore a good grasp of the concept is vital to success.

We encourage you to use this book in conjunction with the Official Florida Vehicle Code, which is available through the Florida DMV's official website or at local DMV offices. The vehicle code contains the most detailed and comprehensive information on Florida's traffic laws and regulations, and it should be consulted whenever you have questions or encounter specific scenarios not covered in this handbook.

Remember, the DMV exam is designed to ensure that you thoroughly understand Florida's driving laws and can apply them safely on the road. Now, let's begin with the questions.

9

EXTRA PREPARATION FOR YOUR TEST

"Success depends upon previous preparation, and without such preparation, there is sure to be failure."

— CONFUCIUS

From wise Confucius, these words ring especially true in your journey toward obtaining your Florida driver's license. The culmination of all your learning and practice is just around the corner. In this chapter, we will ensure that you're fully equipped to pass the Florida DMV exam easily.

The previous chapters laid a solid foundation of knowledge and skills necessary for safe and responsible driving. As the test day looms, it's time to focus on those crucial extra steps that can elevate your preparation to the next level.

We'll delve into proven strategies that make the most of your remaining preparation time.

Feeling a surge of nerves is typical before a significant event like the DMV exam. However, the key is to channel that nervous energy into positive outcomes. This section will explore relaxation techniques, mindfulness practices, and mental exercises to avoid stress and anxiety. By the time you step into the exam room, you'll be armed with the tools to maintain a clear and focused mind.

Simulating the test is one of the most effective ways to assess your readiness. By applying your knowledge and skills in this simulated scenario, you'll identify areas for improvement and build the confidence needed to excel on test day.

As you work through this chapter, you'll find your self-assurance growing. Remember, you've put in the effort, honed your skills, and gained the necessary knowledge. It's time to trust in your preparation.

LAST-MINUTE TIPS AND TECHNIQUES

As the big day approaches, it's time to fine-tune your skills and gather the last-minute tips and techniques that can make all the difference.

Revisiting Crucial Traffic Rules and Road Signs

Before you take the test, take some time to brush up on essential traffic rules and road signs. Review the right-of-way rules, speed limits, and various road signs. This quick review will reinforce your knowledge and boost your confidence when taking the test.

A Good Night's Sleep: Your Secret Weapon

Sleep is your ultimate ally. Make sure to get a solid night's rest before the test day. A well-rested mind is sharper and more focused, allowing you to make split-second decisions and react appropriately to different driving situations. Adequate sleep enhances your cognitive abilities and keeps anxiety at bay.

Fueling Your Body With a Healthy Meal

On the morning of your test, opt for a balanced meal to provide sustained energy. Avoid heavy, greasy foods that might leave you feeling sluggish. A well-fueled body contributes to clearer thinking and increased alertness.

Arriving Early: Set the Tone for Success

Ensure you have ample time for any unexpected delays, which helps calm your nerves. When you're not rushing, you can take a moment to mentally prepare, review your notes, and visualize your success.

TEST TIPS FOR A SUCCESSFUL KNOWLEDGE TEST

Remember, success on the driving test requires practical skills, knowledge, and a composed demeanor. Here are some additional tips that can guide you toward a successful outcome:

- **DMV practice tests:** Familiarize yourself with the DMV practice tests in this book and on the DMV website. They offer valuable insights into the format and types of questions you might encounter.
- **Timing matters:** Wait to take the test until you're truly ready. Ensure you've honed your skills and feel confident in your abilities.

As you prepare for your Florida DMV exam, remember that success results from your dedication, practice, and determination. Approach the test with a clear mind and the knowledge you've put in the effort necessary to pass the exam easily. Trust in your abilities, stay composed, and let your hard work shine through.

MANAGING EXAM STRESS

The knowledge test is a significant milestone, and while a touch of anxiety is typical, managing stress effectively can make a world of difference in your performance. That's why finding ways to channel your nervousness constructively is essential. Let's explore some proven techniques to manage exam stress.

Visualization Techniques

Picture yourself confidently understanding and correctly answering all the exam questions. Visualization not only boosts your confidence but also preps your mind for success.

The Power of a Positive Mindset

Approaching your permit test with a positive mindset is a game-changer. It's not just about thinking positively but about cultivating a mental environment supporting your success. Here are the top ways to infuse positivity into your test day:

- **Tell yourself you're ready:** Remember the countless hours invested in learning and practice. Trust in your preparation and reassure yourself that you're well-equipped to handle the test.
- **Keep it a secret:** Sharing your test day plans with too many people can amplify stress. Keep your circle small and share only with those who provide encouragement and support.
- **Don't skip meals:** A balanced meal fuels your body and mind. Don't skip meals, as it can lead to energy crashes and increased stress. Choose nutrient-rich options that provide sustained energy throughout the day.
- **Pretend it's a mock:** Approach the test as if it were a mock exam. This mindset shift can ease the pressure and allow you to showcase your skills more naturally.

Stay Off the Caffeine

Excess caffeine can intensify nervousness and restlessness. Opt for calming herbal teas instead.

As you approach your Florida DMV exam, remember that managing stress is integral to your preparation. Implement these strategies and think positively to enhance your performance and give you a more enjoyable test experience.

NAVIGATING TEST DAY WITH EASE: AVOIDING STRESS FOR DRIVING SUCCESS

The day of your Florida DMV permit test has arrived, and the mix of excitement and apprehension is typical; however, it's crucial to keep stress at bay for this life-altering examination.

Organize Your Time

Time management is a valuable skill, even on test days. Plan your morning routine in a way that allows you to comfortably get ready without rushing. Allocate sufficient time for meals, dressing, and travel. By keeping a steady pace, you'll enter the test center with a composed and relaxed demeanor.

Breathe

Before you step into the examination area, pause for a moment and Inhale deeply through your nose, hold for a count of four, and then slowly exhale through your mouth. (Greenshield, 2019). This calming breath helps ease nervous tension and centers your focus. Remember that you've prepared diligently and are ready to demonstrate your skills.

Be Confident

Incorporating these stress-relieving techniques into your test day routine allows you to create a more positive and composed experience. Remember, stress is a natural response to significant events, but rest easy knowing you are armed with ways to manage it effectively. Approach your Florida DMV permit test with confidence, clarity, and the knowledge you've put in the effort to be well-prepared.

Operating a vehicle isn't solely reliant on skill; it is also about maintaining a calm and focused state of mind. As you embark on this leg of your journey to becoming a licensed driver, remember these strategies.

MOCK DMV TEST

Congratulations on reaching this stage of your journey to becoming a licensed driver in Florida. To help you gauge your readiness for the upcoming DMV driving test, we've prepared a comprehensive mock test. This test covers a range of topics, including rules of the road, road signs, and defensive driving techniques. Remember, the more you practice, the more confident and prepared you'll be on test day.

The questions provided here are a sample of the types of questions you may encounter on the Florida DMV permit test. The actual test may vary in content and format. Your dedication to practice and preparation is key to achieving success. Best of luck as you move closer to your goal of becoming a licensed driver!

Please select the correct answer for each question.

1. Which of these is a false assumption?

a) You may legally drive 10 miles per hour above the speed limit if on the fast lane.

b) Going above the speed limit is allowed to pass.

c) You cannot be cited for going significantly below the speed limit.

d) All of the above.

2. A flashing yellow light on a Drawbridge means

a) Speed up to assure you get through

b) The bridge is being shut down for mechanical failure

c) Reduce speed and be ready to stop

d) None of the above

3. Choose the correct statement regarding blind spots

a) If you find yourself in another drivers blind spot, move ahead or drop back to get out of the blind spot as soon as safely possible

b) The only way to assure your blind spot is clear is to look over your shoulder

c) Large trucks have more blind spots than regular vehicles

d) All of the above

4. When pulled over by an officer:

a) Pull over to the right, stay in the drivers seat and keep your hands visible

b) You will be asked to provide proof of insurance

c) You will be required to present your driver's license and vehicle registration

d) All of the above

5. The safest way to back up (go in reverse) is:

a) Do it quickly before anyone gets to park behind you

b) Look directly out the front, if it appears straight don't look anywhere else as you will lose the straight position

c) Looking solely on your rearview mirror

d) Look out the rear window looking over your right shoulder

6. For lane changes, it's safest to:

a) Make one lane change at a time

b) maintain your current speed during the lane change

c) Signal in advance of a lane change

d) All of the above

7. Maximum speed limit in Limited Access Highways:

a) 45 mph
b) 50 mph
c) 60 mph
d) 70 mph

8. It is appropriate to use your horn if

a) You see an acquaintance on the opposite side of the street
b) It is to avoid a collision
c) The vehicle in front doesn't immediately go once the light turns green
d) Both a and c

9. Choose the correct statement in regard to passing vehicles:

a) On two lane roads drivers will need to use the oncoming traffic lane to pass
b) Drivers should not assume the driver being passed will make space for the passing vehicle to return
c) It's safe for the passing vehicle to return to their lane once they can see the headlights of the vehicle being passed in their rearview mirror
d) All of the above

10. Who will be cited if you get pulled over and a passenger under 18 in the front seat is not wearing a safety belt?

a) The driver
b) Both the driver and the passenger
c) The passengers school principal
d) Both A and B

11. Drivers shall _____ while driving through a school zone:

a) Obey crossing guards

b) Follow reduced school speed limits

c) Be extra cautious of children crossing

d) All of the above

12. To complete a merge on a reduction of lanes

a) Lower your window and point straight down

b) Stop to make sure it is safe to proceed

c) Activate your hazard lights

d) Perform the maneuver like a lane change using the turn signal, looking at the side mirror, and looking over your shoulder

13. Minimum age to get a learner license (instruction permit)

a) 13

b) 14 1/2

c) 15

d) 15 1/2

14. What are the hour restrictions for 16-year-olds?

a) Not allowed to drive between 9 am and 3 pm

b) Not allowed to drive between 5 pm and 9 pm

c) Not allowed to drive between 11 pm and 6 am

d) Not allowed to drive on the weekends

15. When speed is tripled, the impact force will be:

a) 3 times the amount

b) 5 times the amount

c) 9 times the amount

d) 25 times the amount

16. Red reflectors facing you indicate

a) Preparation for a parade
b) You're driving in the opposite side of traffic
c) That stretch of road doubles as commuter airplane landing strip
d) None of the above

17. What does a red octagonal sign mean?

a) Yield
b) Stop
c) Merge
d) Slow down

18. Which of the following is true in regard to freeway driving:

a) If you miss your exit continue driving and find an alternate route
b) When exiting slow down once you enter the deceleration lane
c) You should make room for merging traffic whenever possible
d) All of the above

19. What are the height bumper requirements for a vehicle weighing less than 2500 pounds:

a) 22 inches in the front, 24 inches in the back
b) 22 inches in both the front and rear
c) 23 inches in the front, 26 inches in the back
d) 25 inches in both the front and rear

20. Recreation area signs are:

a) Orange
b) Purple
c) Brown
d) Yellow

21. When merging onto a freeway, you should:

a) Come to a complete stop before entering the freeway
b) Honk and flash your high beams if you think the other driver is not letting you in
c) Be at or near the speed of traffic and look for a gap to merge smoothly into traffic
d) Both B and C

22. What does a yellow X mean on top of a lane?

a) Lane control is in use, all drivers must vacate lane as it's about to turn red
b) Accident ahead
c) Must have 3 or more occupants to continue
d) There is at least 10 minutes left before it turns red

23. When a traffic signal turns green, you should

a) Accelerate as quickly as possible
b) Yield the right-of-way to pedestrians and vehicles still in the intersection
c) Honk your horn to alert other drivers
d) Change lanes immediately

24. You must use your headlights

a) After 5 in the evening
b) After sunset and before sunrise
c) When driving in heavy traffic
d) When driving on the freeway

25. Regulatory signs are:

a) Pennants with black or red lettering
b) White squares or rectangles with black or red lettering
c) Crossbucks
d) None of the above

26. What should you do if your vehicle's accelerator pedal sticks?

a) Immediately apply the emergency brake to its maximum capability
b) Pump the accelerator pedal vigorously
c) Apply the brakes and shift to neutral
d) Flash your high beams continuously to warn other drivers

27. If involved in a collision, it is unlawful to:

a) Take pictures of the scene
b) Call for assistance
c) Leave the scene
d) Talk to the other party before police or paramedics arrive

28. What actions should you take if you encounter a tire blowout while operating a vehicle?

a) Slam on the brakes
b) Steer sharply to the side of the road
c) Hold the steering wheel firmly and do not use brakes, gradually slow down
d) Shift into neutral and coast to a stop

29. When executing a right turn with a red light, you are required to

a) Come to a complete stop and yield the right-of-way to all other traffic
b) Slow down, but you can turn without stopping
c) Come to a complete stop, flash high beams, and complete the turn
d) Make the turn without stopping if the way is clear

30. What does a yellow diamond-shaped sign with a black arrow pointed at an angle mean?

a) Sharp turn ahead
b) No passing zone
c) Divided highway ahead
d) Warning of a school zone

31. What do white lights mean on the back of a vehicle?

a) Reverse
b) Hazards
c) Warning of traffic congestion ahead
d) None of the above

32. If two vehicles arrive simultaneously to a four-way stop, the vehicle _____ has the right of way:

a) To the left.
b) That honks first.
c) That approaches from the road with the higher speed limit.
d) To the right.

33. A mandate for towing something is:

a) The drawbar must be strong enough to pull the weight
b) Chains must be used
c) Must have a certificate from a reputable dealer for the installation of the drawbar
d) None of the above

34. When there are two lanes that turn together, drivers must:

a) Make eye contact with the other drivers through the turn
b) Begin and end in the lane they started their turn from.
c) Both A and B
d) None of the above

35. Emergency hazard lights are to be used:

a) In shopping centers looking for a place to park
b) When your vehicle is disabled
c) When temporarily disoriented looking for a destination
d) All of the above

36. Which of these is a good idea

a) Don't make a last-minute lane change in front of a commercial truck as they need more distance to stop than passenger vehicles
b) Check your rearview mirror often to know your position among other vehicles
c) When passing a lot of parked vehicles in a row, be ready for one of them to dart into traffic
d) All of the above

37. At all way stops

a) The vehicle that arrives first gets precedent
b) The vehicle from the bigger road gets precedent
c) Electric vehicles and hybrids get precedent
d) Both A and C

38. A slow moving vehicle can be identified by:

a) A white flag that sticks out from the trunk
b) A large flashing light on the back window
c) Orange reflective triangle with a red border
d) None of the above

39. Guide signs are:

a) Blue
b) Brown
c) Green
d) White

40. What is the purpose of a crosswalk with white lines painted across the road?

a) To indicate the end of a no-parking zone

b) To mark lanes for bicycles

c) To indicate where pedestrians may cross the road

d) To create additional lanes for vehicles

41. U-turns are unlawful:

a) If a no U-turn sign is present

b) If you can't see 200 feet ahead

c) At the entrance of a fire station

d) All are correct

42. The following are exempt from seat belt requirements

a) Person delivering newspapers

b) Farm equipment

c) Trucks of net weight of more than 26,000 pounds

d) All of the above

43. What is the minimum age to obtain a regular, _non-probationary_ class E driver's license in Florida?

a) 16 years old

b) 17 years old

c) 18 years old

d) 21 years old

44. You approach an intersection to make a left turn and the green arrow turns into a green light.

a) The turn can still be completed **after** yielding to oncoming traffic
b) Stop behind the line and wait for the next green arrow
c) Continue the turn regardless of oncoming traffic since you entered the lane with a green arrow
d) You must exit turn lane and go straight

45. A winding road sign is:

a) A red arrow, turning left, a second arrow turning right in a yellow diamond
b) A black arrow, winding or squiggly, directed upward within a yellow diamond
c) A black circle within a pentagon sign
d) A black triangle within a diamond

46. What are the 3 categories of distracted driving

a) Visual, Manual, and Cognitive
b) Physical, Transitive, and Imaginative
c) Meditative, Emotional, and Analytical
d) City, Rural and Highway

47. Stopping on the freeway acceleration ramp

a) Is required
b) Should only be done if the freeway traffic is stopped
c) Is allowed with a special pass issued by the department of transportation
d) Both B and C

48. Not wearing seat belts can lead to _____ in a collision

    a) Being ejected from the vehicle
    b) Being thrown against the steering wheel or windshield
    c) Losing total control of the vehicle
    d) All of the above

49. How is the railroad sign depicted?

    a) Star
    b) Pentagon
    c) Octagon
    d) Circle or Crossbuck

50. The following must be given the right of way

    a) Youth sport buses
    b) Nonresponding emergency vehicles
    c) Student driver vehicles
    d) Funeral processions

Answers
1. d 2. c 3. d 4. d 5. d 6. d 7. d 8. b 9. d 10. a
11. d 12. d 13. c 14. c 15. c 16. b 17. b 18. d 19. a 20. c
21. c 22. A 23. b 24. b 25. b 26. c 27. c 28. c 29. a 30. a
31. a 32. d 33. a 34. b 35. b 36. d 37. a 38. c 39. c 40. c
41. d 42. d 43. c 44. a 45. b 46. a 47. b 48. d 49. d 50. d

PRACTICE EXAM 1

It's time to put your knowledge to the test with these practice exams. Remember, this mirrors what you might face on the actual DMV test. Let's get started!

INSTRUCTIONS:

- Ensure you are in a quiet space where you won't be disturbed.
- Have a pencil or pen and a piece of paper handy to jot down your answers.
- Read each question carefully. Consider every detail as it might lead you to the correct answer.
- Do not rush. Though the actual DMV exam is timed, this practice test isn't. Be sure to allow yourself time to comprehend each question prior to selecting an answer.
- Once you've tackled all questions, proceed to the Answer Key to check how you've done.
- Review any questions you got wrong and make sure you understand the correct answer to avoid repeating the same mistake in the future.

PRACTICE EXAM

1. A solid green arrow at an intersection signifies:

    a) No U turns allowed
    b) Drivers can turn in the direction of the arrow if safe to do so
    c) Drivers can legally exit the turn lane and continue straight
    d) None of the above

2. A red and white sign with a downward triangular shape means

    a) Yield the right-of-way
    b) Stop ahead
    c) No right on red
    d) Railroad crossing ahead

3. Drivers are to _____ prior to proceeding if behind a school bus that has flashing red lights and an extended stop sign.

    a) Lower their window and yell their intentions
    b) Stop and wait for the lights to stop flashing and for the stop sign to be retracted
    c) Flash their high beams and honk their horn
    d) Stop, wait 3 seconds, and look both ways

4. A yield sign means as you approach, you must:

    a) Flash your high beams
    b) Slow down and be prepared to stop if necessary to give the right-of-way
    c) Merge into traffic without stopping
    d) Speed up to merge quickly

5. When parking on a downhill slope, you should turn your wheels

a) Toward the curb away from the road
b) Toward the road
c) Parallel to the curb
d) It doesn't matter

6. If you are involved in a collision, you must exchange information with the other party. What information should you provide?

a) Your name, driver's license, proof of insurance, and vehicle registration.
b) Your name and insurance information only.
c) Your driver's license number and phone number.
d) Your name and nothing else.

7. To avoid glare from high beams of an approaching vehicle, you should:

a) Look to the right side of the road
b) Look to the left side of the road
c) Look straight ahead
d) Turn on your high beams

8. _____ is the minimum following distance in normal weather conditions:

a) 8 seconds
b) 6 seconds
c) 4 seconds
d) 2 seconds

9. A shared lane marking:

a) Helps cyclists with lateral positioning
b) Alert drivers of the location cyclists are likely to be
c) Encourage drivers to pass cyclists safely
d) All of the above

10. What should you do when you approach a roundabout?

a) Proceed in a clockwise direction
b) Yield to pedestrians or traffic already in the roundabout
c) Watch for vehicles from the right who have the right of way
d) All are correct

11. Reaction distance:

a) Does not factor when needing to come to a stop.
b) Is the distance a vehicle covers from the moment the driver recognizes the need to respond to the point where the driver initiates action.
c) Is a lot better if driving sports cars.
d) Refers to a pedestrian reacting to your vehicle

12. When parallel parking, you should be within _____ from the curb:

a) 18 inches
b) 12 inches
c) 2 feet
d) 3 feet

13. What is the minimum age to apply for a Class "E" driver's license in Florida?

a) 16 years old
b) 17 years old
c) 18 years old
d) 21 years old

14. What should you do if, as you approach a railroad crossing, it starts flashing red lights and its gates are lowered?

a) Stop and wait until the lights stop flashing and the gates are raised
b) If you think you can make it speed up, the train must yield to you
c) Cross the tracks if no train is visible
d) Honk your horn and proceed

15. If your car _does not_ have Anti-lock brakes (ABS)

a) Pump your brakes
b) Accelerate
c) Press and hold the brake down
d) Press the brake and accelerator at the same time

16. What is the maximum BAC limit for drivers 21 and older?

a) 0.08%
b) 0.01%
c) 0.10%
d) Any level as long as the person is coherent

17. When driving in foggy conditions, you should:

  a) Slow down and use high beams
  b) Slow down and use low beams
  c) Stick your head out the window
  d) None of the above

18. _____ to indicate a left turn.

  a) Extend your left arm and hand upward
  b) Extend your left arm and hand horizontally
  c) Extend your right arm and hand upward
  d) Extend your right arm and hand horizontally

19. Children under the age of _____ must be in a safety seat:

  a) 8
  b) 7
  c) 4
  d) 5

20. This is a sign your brakes are likely in need of repair:

  a) The brake pedal doesn't rest well above the floor
  b) The car pulls to one side when you brake
  c) You hear scraping or squealing noises when you brake
  d) All of the above

21. If _there is_ a curb when parking uphill, what should the position of your front wheels be:

  a) Turned away from the curb
  b) Turned toward the curb
  c) Straight and parallel to the curb
  d) Turned left

22. A pedestrian that utilizes a white cane or guide dog:

a) Will give the drivers hand signs on whether to proceed or not
b) Is expected to wait for the intersection to clear prior to crossing
c) Will wait for drivers verbal instructions
d) Is to be given the right of way

23. Drivers can go back to the road speed limit in school zones when:

a) They don't see a crossing guard
b) There are no other vehicles to obstruct your view of children
c) They reach the "End of school zone" sign
d) There are no school buses up ahead

24. Drivers are to signal their intention to turn at least _____ feet before making the turn.

a) 400 feet
b) 350 feet
c) 50 feet
d) 100 feet

25. When making a lane change from a slower speed lane to a faster one, you should:

a) Assure the gap between cars is large enough and begin accelerating while performing the lane change
b) Assure the gap between cars is large enough and maintain your current speed while performing the lane change
c) Assure the gap between cars is large enough and slow down while performing the lane change
d) None of the above

26.The best thing to do if someone cuts you off:

    a) Don't take it personal

    b) Pass them and cut them off yourself

    c) Flash your high beams at them

    d) Tailgate them to voice your frustration until they change lanes or apologize

27. If you are approaching a railroad crossing with no warning signals or gates, you should:

    a) Speed up to cross the tracks quickly

    b) Reduce speed and prepare to stop if necessary

    c) Continue at the same speed

    d) Change lanes to avoid the tracks

28. In the event a driver fails to for a school bus with flashing red lights and an extended stop sign, the repercussion is?

    a) A warning

    b) Car impounded for 10 days

    c) A $265 fine and possible suspension of your driver's license

    d) 2 year jail time

29. When drivers arrive simultaneously at uncontrolled (blind) intersections, the driver _____ has the right of way.

    a) With the smaller car

    b) To the right

    c) To the left

    d) Coming in with lesser speed

30. How close to an intersection can you park?

a) 20 feet
b) 10 feet
c) 50 feet
d) 100 feet

31. A driver should _____ when driving at night or when there is low visibility:

a) Drive faster than usual
b) Use their hazard lights and flash high beams
c) Increase their following distance
d) All of the above

32. It's important to remember to _____ approaching a curve:

a) Increase your speed
b) Keep your speed constant
c) Reduce speed
d) Switch lanes to pass slower vehicles

33. Which of the following statements about parking in a handicapped parking space is true?

a) You can park in a handicapped space if you'll only be there for a few minutes
b) You can park in a handicapped space if you have a disabled family member with you
c) You can park in a handicapped space if you display a disabled placard or license plate
d) You can park in a handicapped space if you are driving a rental car

34. When should a three-point turn be done

a) If the road is too narrow for a U turn and you can't go around the block
b) During daytime hours
c) both A and B
d) In front of schools

35. Stripes on a barricade sloping downward right mean:

a) Uneven road
b) Do a U turn
c) Traffic should flow to the left
d) Traffic should flow to the right

36. It is _____ to do a lane change while going through an intersection.

a) Safe
b) Illegal
c) Legal while the sun is out
d) None of the above

37. Which of the following is true about pedestrians?

a) The right-of-way must always be given to pedestrians at crosswalks
b) They are to be given the right-of-way when crossing at unmarked crosswalks
c) Drivers must wait until they finish crossing even when they enter the crosswalk once the "Don't walk" sign has been activated
d) All of the above

38. When using your high beams, you should switch to low beams at _____ of an approaching vehicle.

    a) 1000 feet
    b) 500 feet
    c) 1500 feet
    d) None are correct

39. When you see a solid yellow line on your side of the road, it means

    a) You may pass if the way is clear
    b) You may pass with caution
    c) You can cross it to make a left turn
    d) You may pass if you are in a hurry

40. A "safe speed" is best described as

    a) It's basic knowledge that the fast lane on the freeway is to speed
    b) A speed that allows you to remain in control to avoid collisions
    c) It is basic knowledge that the slow lane is to drive significantly below the posted speed limit
    d) You may drive above the posted speed limit if you are passing another vehicle

41. Which of the following is true about a flashing red traffic light?

    a) Treat it like a stop sign
    b) Slow down and proceed with caution
    c) Speed up and proceed through the intersection
    d) It has no special meaning

42. A bicyclist ahead extends their left hand and points downward, they are

a) Slowing down or stopping
b) Making a right turn
c) Turning left
d) None of the above

43. A yellow sign with a black semi-truck on a steep grade means

a) Runaway ramp ahead
b) Truck rest stop ahead
c) Steep hill ahead
d) EV charging station ahead

44. To be safe while passing a bicyclist:

a) Sound your horn
b) Accelerate to quickly pass them
c) Leave at least three feet of space while passing them
d) Pass them only if they signal you to do so

45. What do dashed white lines in the middle of a two lane road indicate?

a) Passing is allowed
b) It is a one-way street
c) Both A and B
d) It is a two-way street

46. What does a yellow turn sign with the number 35 on it mean?

a) The recommended speed is 35 for the turn but as a defensive driver reduce your speed to 20
b) Turn at whatever the official speed limit is for the road
c) The road turns in the direction of the arrow and reduce speed to the number indicated
d) None of the above

47. When driving in heavy rain:

a) Use your high beams to improve visibility
b) Increase your speed to get through it more quickly
c) Reduce your speed, turn on your headlights, and increase following distance
d) Follow closely behind the vehicle in front of you

48. Which educational course must you complete when applying for a learner's permit (or if you have never possessed a driver's license):

a) Vehicle value guide
b) Vehicle maintenance
c) Traffic Law and Substance Abuse
d) None of the above

49. These are commonly used channelizing devices:

a) Drums
b) Barricades
c) Vertical panels
d) All of the above

50. If you are the driver or owner of a vehicle at fault in a crash and you're not insured in compliance with the Financial Responsibility law:

a) Receive a warning
b) Get a small fine
c) You may be mandated to pay the damages prior to your driving privilege being restored
d) None of the above

Practice Exam 1: Answer Sheet

1. b) 2. a) 3. b) 4. b) 5. a) 6. a) 7. a) 8. c) 9. d) 10. b)
11. b) 12. b) 13. a) 14. a) 15. a) 16. a) 17. b) 18. b) 19. d) 20. d)
21. a) 22. d) 23. c) 24. d) 25. a) 26. a) 27. b) 28. c) 29. b) 30. a)
31. c) 32. c) 33. c) 34. a) 35. d) 36. b) 37. d) 38. b) 39. c) 40. b)
41. a) 42. a) 43. c) 44. c) 45. c) 46. c) 47. c) 48. c) 49. d) 50. c)

PRACTICE EXAM 2

1. If an officer suspects your vehicle is not properly maintained and is unsafe to be on the road

    a) They can stop that vehicle at any time
    b) Can take the license plate down and write a letter to the owner of what is concerning
    c) Must give the driver 15 days notice prior to inspecting the vehicle
    d) None of the above

2. Which is true regarding emergency vehicles:

    a) They are to be given the right of way at all times if using flashing lights
    b) If you are crossing or in an intersection as the emergency vehicle approaches, continue through to the other side
    c) Change lanes if passing on the lane next to a responding emergency vehicle, if not able to change lanes reduce speed to 20 mph
    d) All of the above

3. A merge sign:

a) A sign in the shape of a yellow diamond featuring a black arrow pointing upward, with another arrow merging into the center of the first arrow
b) A sign in the shape of a yellow circle featuring a black arrow pointing downward, with another arrow merging into the center of the first arrow
c) A sign in the shape of a blue triangle featuring a black arrow pointing upward, with another arrow pointing downward
d) None of the above

4. You are legally required to _____ when an emergency vehicle, using a siren and red lights, approaches you.

a) Honk your horn
b) Pull over and stop
c) Increase your speed
d) Proceed as usual

5. For safety, drivers should _____ when freeway driving:

a) Try to follow the car in front as closely as possible
b) Look further ahead than when on city streets
c) Drive a little faster than everyone else
d) All of the above

6. When being passed by another vehicle, you should

a) Activate high beams to alert oncoming drivers you're being passed
b) Adjust your speed to allow to be passed safely
c) Speed up to avoid being passed
d) Both A and B

7. A green arrow and a red light at a traffic signal means?

a) Stop
b) Yield to oncoming traffic
c) Proceed in the direction of the arrow if it's safe to do so
d) Prepare to make a U-turn

8. A driver should _____ to avoid collisions

a) Assume other drivers will adhere to driving rules
b) Speed up crossing intersections
c) Yield their right-of-way
d) Flash high beams upon approaching intersections

9. Points from traffic convictions stay on your record for

a) 12 months
b) 18 months
c) 24 months
d) 36 months

10. Which is true regarding trains and railroad tracks.

a) Because of their size they appear to be moving slower than they actually are
b) If stopped at multi track railroad crossings, don't proceed until you have a clear view of all the tracks
c) If your vehicle stalls on a track, exit immediately
d) All of the above

11. A right on red is prohibited when:

a) There is a red arrow in that direction
b) A sign prohibits it
c) Both A and B
d) It is raining

12. When passing another vehicle

a) You should make gestures letting the driver you're passing know they have to go faster
b) You should accelerate as much as possible to quickly get back in your lane regardless of the speed limit
c) It is not permitted to drive above the speed limit
d) Both A and B

13. Children between these ages must be in a safety seat or booster

a) 6 and 7
b) 5 and 6
c) 4 and 5
d) 6 and 8

14. Depressants

a) Cause the central nervous system to speed up
b) Slow down the central nervous system
c) Do not have any effect on the central nervous system
d) Cause hallucinations

15. Studies have shown this is the most common citation for drivers between 15 and 19 years of age:

a) Speeding
b) Not wearing seatbelts
c) Using their phones to text or watch videos
d) None of the above

16. Drivers under 18 who accumulate six or more points within a 12 month period

a) Get an Important Trips Only restriction
b) Must have a parent letter dated the day they drive
c) Get a business purposes only restriction
d) Both A and B

17. A minor may lose his or her license with this amount of alcohol in the body:

a) 0.04%
b) 0.05%
c) 0.08%
d) 0.02%

18. Malfunctioning traffic lights:

a) Always have a police officer directing traffic
b) Require you to flash your high beams and honk your horn on approach
c) Are to be treated as yield signs
d) Are to be treated as all way stops

19. Large flashing arrow panels mean?

a) Stop and go in reverse
b) Make a U turn
c) Move into the lane in the direction of the arrows
d) Stop in the lane

20. If you encounter an animal on the road, the best action is to

a) Accelerate to scare it away
b) Turn sharply to avoid it
c) Drive cautiously and if there is an animal on the road, wait for it to clear on its own
d) Honk your horn to scare it away

21. Pedestrians should

a) Follow traffic laws
b) Wear reflective clothing
c) Walk in the direction against traffic
d) All of the above

22. Alcohol affects:

a) Judgement
b) Reaction time
c) Driving skills
d) All of the above

23. It is unlawful to

a) Damage roads by driving on rims with flat tires or any other means of damage
b) Drive with headlights on during the day
c) Use a low gear driving up a steep incline

d) All of the above

24. If an object's speed doubles, what is the effect on the object's force of impact?

a) No change
b) It is increased twofold
c) Four times
d) Depends on its mass

25. What are the hour restrictions for 17-year-olds?

a) Not allowed to drive between 9 am and 5 pm
b) Not allowed to drive between 1 am and 5 am
c) Not allowed to drive between 11 pm and 6 am
d) Not allowed to drive on the weekends

26. If you pass a school bus and cause injuries:

a) You will get a $1500 fine and 6 points added to your driving record
b) Have your drivers license suspended
c) Possible community service and mandatory driver improvement course
d) All of the above

27. In what situations can your driver's license face suspension?

a) DUI
b) Passing a school bus
c) Evading arrest
d) All of the above

28. Passing is not allowed:

a) On 3 lane highways
b) Once the sun has gone down
c) If you have to drive off the roadway to pass
d) If within 500 feet of a traffic light

29. Which is true regarding rain:

a) For better traction you should try to turn sharper than normal
b) The roads being wet have no effect on control
c) Roads are the most slippery the first 30 minutes after a long dry spell
d) None of the above

30. If you approach a vehicle from the rear with your high beams on, at what distance do you need to switch them to your regular beams?

a) 1000 feet
b) 300 feet
c) 100 feet
d) ¾ mile

31. The appropriate action for a solid yellow light at an intersection:

a) Slow down and stop if safe to do so
b) Speed up to beat the light
c) turn on emergency hazards
d) Stop at all costs prior to entering the intersection

32. The risk of hydroplaning can be lessened by:

a) Increasing speed
b) Continually accelerating quickly and trying to stop quickly
c) Reducing your speed
d) None of the above

33. A three-point turn should not be done:

a) On hills
b) If a U turn is not allowed
c) On a highway
d) All of the above

34. Following the flow of traffic means

a) Drive as fast as everyone else, no matter if it is above the speed limit, or you will be cited for going too slow
b) Take your foot off the accelerator when going downhill and cruise to save fuel
c) You should pass anyone doing less than the speed limit
d) Within reason, drive at approximately the same speed as everyone else

35. Common causes of car crashes include

a) Exceeding the speed limit
b) Making an improper turn
c) Violating the right-of-way rules
d) All of the above

36. What does BAC stand for?

a) Blood Alcohol Control
b) Blood Alcohol Count
c) Blood Alcohol Casualty
d) Blood Alcohol Content

37. To get a learner's permit, every applicant must pass a vision test and a _____.

a) Practical driving test
b) Vehicle inspection test
c) Knowledge test
d) Medical examination

38. What does a solid white line in the middle of a two lane road indicate?

a) Passing is not allowed
b) It is a one-way street
c) Both A and B
d) It is a two-way street

39. All vehicle rear stop lights must be _____:

a) White
b) Orange
c) Red
d) Brown

40. What is utilized to judge distance between yourself and other objects:

a) Lateral vision
b) Depth perception
c) Multi view perception
d) Forced perception

41. A curb painted green means

a) Parking for a limited time, a sign usually displays the time allowed
b) Parking for an unlimited time
c) Parking for compact vehicles only
d) All of the above

42. A curb painted yellow means

a) Parking for passenger vehicles only
b) Parking for freight unloading; the driver must remain with the vehicle
c) Parking for emergency vehicles
d) All of the above

43. A blue-painted curb signifies parking allowed

a) For residents only
b) For handicapped parking only
c) For commercial vehicles only
d) For motorcycles only

44. A no passing sign is:

a) A pennant
b) An octagon
c) A hexagon
d) A circle

45. A change of address must be completed within _____.

a) 12 days
b) 72 hours
c) 30 days
d) 48 hours

46. An effect of your brakes having gotten wet by driving through a large puddle

a) May pull to one side when braking
b) Brakes may not respond with same efficiency
c) Both A and B
d) None are correct

47. To make a right turn, you should

a) Stay behind any bicyclists
b) Slow to a safe speed and signal at least 100 feet prior to the maneuver
c) Yield to pedestrians and bicyclists prior to entering the intersection
d) All of the above

48. Parents need to be alert to the following dangers involving cars and infants:

a) Forgetting an infant in a hot car
b) Forgetting to check behind the vehicle prior to reversing to assure a child is not behind the vehicle
c) Having an unnoticed infant getting in an unoccupied vehicle and not be able to get out on a hot day
d) All of the above

49. Does the displayed speed limit of 55 mph signify that you are permitted to drive at 55 mph on that highway under any circumstance?

a) Only if in the fast lane
b) Yes, otherwise you can be cited for holding traffic back
c) No, speed shall be adjusted for road conditions
d) Yes, during daylight hours

50. What does a red X mean on top of a lane?

a) Passing is allowed if safe
b) Lane control is in use – don't enter
c) The road is under construction
d) A pedestrian crosswalk

Practice Exam 2: Answer Sheet
1. a) 2. d) 3. a) 4. b) 5. b) 6. b) 7. c) 8. c) 9. d) 10. d)
11. c) 12. c) 13. c) 14. b) 15. a) 16. c) 17. d) 18. d) 19. c) 20. c)
21. d) 22. d) 23. a) 24. c) 25. b) 26. d) 27. d) 28. c) 29. c) 30. b)
31. a) 32. c) 33. d) 34. d) 35. d) 36. d) 37. c) 38. c) 39. c) 40. b)
41. a) 42. b) 43. b) 44. a) 45. c) 46. c) 47. d) 48. d) 49. c) 50. b)

PRACTICE EXAM 3

1. What does an orange sign with black lettering indicate?

    a) A school zone
    b) Work/Construction zone
    c) A hospital zone
    d) A scenic route

2. Maximum speed within a school zone:

    a) 15 mph
    b) 30 mph
    c) 10 mph
    d) 20 mph

3. Which is true regarding driving through work zones?

    a) Must obey the directions of a flag person
    b) Must follow reduced speed limits
    c) Delays are common
    d) All of the above

4. The hand gesture to indicate "stop" is:

a) Extend your left hand out the driver's side window and move it up and down
b) Point your left hand downward out the driver's side window
c) Extend your left hand straight out the driver's side window
d) Waive your left hand in a circular motion outside the driver's side window

5. Texting and driving:

a) Is encouraged
b) Clears your mind
c) Is normally not a factor in collisions
d) Is not allowed

6. A school sign is:

a) A pennant
b) A pentagon
c) An elongated diamond
d) A circle

7. It is illegal to park within _____ of a stop, traffic or flashing signal

a) 100 feet
b) 50 feet
c) 30 feet
d) 15 feet

8. Each car must have:

a) two braking systems
b) horn
c) side and rearview mirrors
d) All of the above

9. Driving in this condition is dangerous

a) Angry
b) Extremely nervous
c) Emotionally upset
d) All of the above

10. Minimum insurance amounts acceptable in Florida?

a) $12,500 Personal Injury Protection (PIP) and $7,500
Property Damage Protection (PDP)
b) $30,000 Personal Injury Protection (PIP) and $15,000
Property Damage Protection (PDP)
c) $15,000 Personal Injury Protection (PIP) and $15,000
Property Damage Protection (PDP)
d) $10,000 Personal Injury Protection (PIP) and $10,000
Property Damage Protection (PDP)

11. If your car has Anti-Lock Brakes (ABS) and you begin to skid

a) Pump your brakes
b) Accelerate
c) Press and hold the brake down
d) Press the brake and accelerator at the same time

12. Left turns from multilane one-way streets onto a one-way street should be started from what lane?

a) The farthest left
b) Any middle lane
c) The farthest right
d) Any lane

13. If you approach an intersection with a green light but notice it is not clear of traffic, you should

a) Proceed quickly to avoid holding up traffic
b) Stay out of the intersection until it clears
c) Honk your horn to alert other drivers
d) Flash your headlights to signal the right-of-way

14. Driving significantly below the speed limit:

a) Is a cornerstone of defensive driving
b) Is unlawful
c) Shows maturity
d) Earns insurance discounts

15. The fine associated with exceeding the speed limit by more than 50 mph:

a) $250
b) $500
c) More than $1000
d) $750

16. Minimum tire depth:

a) The size of a .25 cent coin
b) 9/10 of an inch
c) one inch
d) 3/32 of an inch

17. You approach an intersection with a red light, and there is a police officer who is in the intersection and waves you to proceed. What should you do?

a) Follow the police officer's instructions and go through even though the light is red
b) Stop and point out to the police officer the danger of waving you through with a red light
c) Stop and wait for the light to turn green
d) Speed up to show you clearly are following the officer's instructions

18. If you're mandated to have higher insurance coverage limits but cannot furnish proof of the elevated limits, you will:

a) Pay a small fine
b) Have to get out of state insurance
c) Have your driver's license and plates suspended up to three years
d) Have your driver's license and plates suspended up to five

19. A passenger having an open alcoholic container:

a) Is lawful
b) Is unlawful
c) Is lawful if the passenger is 21 or older
d) Is lawful if the passenger is sleeping

20. The consequence for littering up to 15 pounds:

a) $250 fine
b) $150 fine
c) $100 fine
d) None of the above

21. A DUI stays on your record:

a) 5 years
b) 10 years
c) 75 years
d) 25 years

22. What is the significance of the speed indicated by speed limit signs?

a) It is non negotiable and must be adhered to in any weather condition
b) It's the maximum legal speed in ideal conditions
c) You can legally drive a few miles above the posted limit if it's an empty open road
d) Both A and C

23. If you feel too tired:

a) Use your fingers to keep your eyes open
b) Get yourself angry
c) Listening to upbeat music
d) Pull over and rest

24. Which of these is a danger to watch out for when driving in neighborhoods:

a) Children that could rush into the street
b) Drivers backing up into the street from their driveways
c) Drivers leaving the curb to join the street unexpectedly
d) All of the above

25. It's a good idea to increase the following distance when following a motorcycle:

a) Because you need room to stop should they fall
b) They can stop a lot quicker than regular vehicles
c) Both a and b
d) Only if the motorcyclist seems to be having difficulty with its handling

26. This sign alerts drivers to slow down before entering a bridge:

a) Dark bridge ahead
b) Slippery bridge ahead
c) Narrow bridge ahead
d) Multiple lane bridge ahead

27. What does a single dashed yellow line in the middle of a two lane road indicate?

a) Passing is allowed
b) It is a two-way street
c) Both A and B
d) It is a one-way street

28. Drowsy driving has this effect:

a) Slows reaction time
b) Impairs Judgement
c) Affects senses
d) All of the above

29. A way to reduce accidents is

a) Focusing solely on the right of way
b) Communicate appropriately
c) Always driving slower than everyone else
d) Constantly changing lanes to try to get ahead

30. A commercial semi-truck ahead of you has signaled that it will turn right. The truck may have to

a) Make a left turn instead
b) Swing wide left first to generate enough space to complete the right turn
c) Stop in the middle of the intersection
d) Turn right without any issues

31. It is illegal to:

a) Leave a 6-year-old child alone in a vehicle
b) Leave a vehicle with its engine running unattended
c) Change lanes into the opposite side of traffic on two lane roads to safely pass a bicyclist
d) Both A and B

32. If your turn signal stops working, you must use hand signals: _____ to indicate a right turn.

a) Stick your right hand out of the window and point straight up
b) Point the left hand straight up out the driver's side.
c) Wave your hand in a circle
d) Stick the right hand out the window and point straight down

33. If involved in a minor collision with no injuries:

a) If possible get off the road and get to the shoulder to keep traffic flowing
b) Don't move the vehicle
c) Open all doors to make it seem bigger for approaching traffic in the lane
d) B and C

34. _____ are required to stop prior to crossing railroad tracks.

a) Bicycles and motorcycles
b) Passenger cars
c) School Buses and vehicles carrying hazardous or flammable materials
d) Electric vehicles

35. When you tailgate other drivers

a) You can irritate the other driver leading to road rage
b) You increase your chances of a collision by reducing your safety buffer
c) You encourage them to speed up
d) Both A and B

36. Drivers must _____ for a red traffic light

a) Come to a complete stop behind the limit line
b) Stop behind the crosswalk
c) Stop prior to entering the intersection
d) All of the above

37. Distracted Driving:

a) Is a factor in a lot of accidents
b) Is an extremely dangerous activity
c) Is something that can be prevented
d) All of the above

38. The elements required to stop are

a) Reaction, perception, and stopping distance
b) Inertia, gravity, and wind speed
c) Time of day, weight of vehicle, and type of road
d) All of the above

39. When driving behind large semi-trucks

a) Stay very close to reduce wind resistance
b) Keep a following distance of greater than four seconds as your view of what is happening ahead is obstructed.
c) Only rely on their brake lights for you to slow down yourself
d) All of the above

40. Flashing yellow lights at intersections mean

a) Proceed at the posted speed limit
b) Slow down and proceed with caution
c) Speed up to get through the intersection before the lights change

d) Stop immediately and wait for further instructions

41. It is illegal to park within _____ of a fire hydrant

a) 3 feet
b) 12 feet
c) 15 feet
d) 30 feet

42. _____ are not allowed on front windshield unless mandated by law:

a) Signs
b) Posters
c) Stickers
d) All of the above

43. What is the minimum field of vision allowed on the vision test?

a) 90 degrees
b) 130 degrees
c) 45 degrees
d) 180 degrees

44. What should you do if you see a train approaching as you approach an uncontrolled railroad crossing?

a) Stop before the crossing and wait for the train to finish going through
b) Stop on the tracks
c) Stop, exit the vehicle, and waive at the train conductor to establish your right-of-way
d) Speed up to beat the train

45. When the pedestrian High Intensity Activated Crosswalk (HAWK) flashes yellow:

a) Speed up to cross before it turns red
b) It is malfunctioning, you can ignore it
c) Reduce speed and be ready to stop, it is about to turn solid red for a pedestrian to cross
d) Pull over to the side of the road

46. What must drivers do when it rains?

a) Turn off their headlights
b) Use windshield wipers and turn on headlights
c) Drive faster to get out of the rain
d) Use the hazard lights instead of headlights

47. A center turn lane can be used for how many feet to complete a left turn?

a) 50 feet
b) 100 feet
c) 200 feet
d) 300 feet

48. Left turns on red lights are permitted_____:

a) Whenever the other drivers signal for you to go
b) Only if no other vehicles are present
c) When turning from a one-way street onto another one-way street
d) Only during nighttime hours

49. It is unlawful to pass (drive on the left half) within _____ of a bridge, viaduct or underground passage:

a) 1000 feet
b) 400 feet
c) 100 feet
d) 200 feet

50. It is unlawful to follow an emergency vehicle closer than

a) 250 feet
b) 350 feet
c) 400 feet
d) 500 feet

Practice Exam 3: Answer Sheet
1. b) 2. d) 3. d) 4. b) 5. d) 6. b) 7. c) 8. d) 9 d) 10. d)
11. c) 12. a) 13. b) 14. b) 15. c) 16. d) 17. a) 18. c) 19. b) 20. b)
21. c) 22. b) 23. d) 24. d) 25. c) 26. c) 27. c) 28. d) 29. b) 30. b)
31. d) 32. b) 33. a) 34. c) 35. d) 36. d) 37. d) 38. a) 39. b) 40. b)
41. c) 42. d) 43. b) 44. a) 45. c) 46. b) 47. c) 48. c) 49. c) 50. d)

PRACTICE EXAM 4

1. The consequences that individuals 21 years of age or older face if convicted of Driving Under the Influence of Alcohol:

a) Fine of $500 to $1,000 (BAL above .15 or minor in the vehicle, minimum fine $1,000 but not more than $2,000), 50 hours community service, up to one-year probation and possible incarceration up to 6 months (if BAL above .15 or minor in the vehicle, up to 9 months).

b) Fine of $1,000 to $1,500 (BAL above .15 or minor in the vehicle, minimum fine $2,000 but not more than $2,500), 75 hours community service, up to 90-day probation and possible incarceration up to 9 months (if BAL above .15 or minor in the vehicle, up to 12 months).

c) Fine of $2,000 to $4,000 (BAL above .09 or minor in the vehicle, minimum fine $3,000 but less than $5,000), 1200 hours community service, up to 5-year probation and possible incarceration up to 2 years (if BAL above .15 or minor in the vehicle, up to 36 months).

d) None of the above.

2. What is true about Motorcycles:

a) They are allowed to ride on sidewalks
b) Are not allowed to take a full parking space at parking lots
c) Have the right to a full driving lane
d) Are prohibited from being driven in the rain

3. Drivers are to stop when approaching a railroad crossing equipped with warning lights but no gates and _____:

    a) The road is wet
    b) You see a green light
    c) The warning lights are flashing red
    d) It is nighttime

4. When encountering a solid yellow line next to a dashed yellow line:

    a) Passing is allowed in both directions during the day
    b) Motorcycles can pass in either direction
    c) Traffic next to the solid yellow can pass
    d) Traffic next to the dashed yellow can pass

5. DUI laws are applicable to:

    a) Alcohol above the legal limit
    b) Illegal drugs
    c) Over the counter and prescription drugs that prohibit driving
    d) All of the above

6. Which statement is true regarding bicycle riders?

    a) They have no rights or responsibilities
    b) They have the same rights and responsibilities as car drivers
    c) They have more rights than car drivers
    d) They have fewer rights than car drivers

7. _____ is a defensive driving technique:

    a) Adjusting speed based on weather/visibility
    b) Looking both ways approaching intersections
    c) Having an escape route

d) All of the above

8. These vehicles can use the HOV lane:

a) High oversize vehicle
b) Vehicles with two or more occupants
c) Hybrid/low emission vehicles
d) Both B and C

9. What is the penalty for refusing to comply with a chemical test of your blood alcohol content when arrested for drunk driving?

a) A fine
b) Driver's license is suspended
c) Required to attend traffic school
d) Receive a warning

10. By signing your drivers license in the state of Florida you agree to implied consent, this means:

a) You choose whether you want local or state penalties if cited
b) You have the right to refuse a chemical test if pulled by law enforcement
c) You agree to a test by law enforcement for the presence of drugs or alcohol
d) You have the right to delay your chemical test by 12 hours unless you were in a collision

11. You intend to make a left turn and have a flashing yellow arrow:

a) Left turn allowed but must wait for arrow to flash green
b) Left turn is allowed but must yield to oncoming traffic
c) Proceed immediately you have a protected left turn

d) The traffic light is not working, proceed as if it was an all-way stop

12. _____ prior to starting the engine:

a) Put on seat belt.
b) Adjust seat position.
c) Adjust side and rear view mirror.
d) All of the above.

13. Traffic fines in construction zones are usually _____

a) Cut in half
b) Charged the same amount as any citation
c) Charged at four times the amount
d) Charged at twice the amount

14. What is the recommended course of action if you exit a freeway and encounter a downhill curved exit ramp?

a) Speed up to merge quickly
b) Slow to a safe speed before the curve
c) Maintain the same speed
d) Use your emergency brake

15. What is a driver required to do with an ignition interlock device?

a) Input the driving route of the driver so authorities always know their location.
b) Take a breath test for alcohol each time the vehicle is started
c) Have fingerprint taken before starting the vehicle
d) Input the number of drinks taken into the device

16. If a person has consumed too much alcohol, among the choices provided, which one will help their body's alcohol metabolism sober up?

    a) Having at least 3 cups of coffee
    b) Having several energy drinks
    c) Taking a cold shower
    d) Only time

17. This dangerous condition happens when driving long distances on monotonous roads:

    a) Highway 101
    b) Route 66
    c) Highway hypnosis
    d) 4-wheel hallucination

18. To whom should you give the right-of-way when waiting to make a left turn?

    a) Cars coming from the opposite direction
    b) Oncoming vehicles turning right
    c) Pedestrians
    d) All of the above

19. If you approach an area that has orange construction signs and traffic cones, you should

    a) Speed up to get through the construction zone quickly
    b) Ignore the signs and continue as usual
    c) Be prepared for workers and slow-moving equipment
    d) Pull over to the side of the road

20. What is the distance at which a load extends beyond your car and needs to be marked by a red flag?

   a) 18 inches
   b) 5 feet
   c) 4 feet
   d) 3 feet

21. A lot of automotive accidents occur:

   a) Between 9 am and 4 pm
   b) At intersections
   c) While on lunch breaks
   d) After three years of driving

22. When there is a large amount of water on the road and it is deeply flooded, it is best to:

   a) Speed up to cross the water as safely as possible
   b) Turn around, do not cross deep water
   c) Exit the vehicle and step in it to determine how deep it truly is
   d) Stop and wait to see what other drivers do

23. "No Zones" are:

   a) Areas not allowed to drive
   b) Areas not allowed to park
   c) Large blind spots on larger vehicles
   d) Only applicable if flashing

24. Steps when changing lanes?

a) Turn signal and rearview mirror
b) Turn signal and side mirrors
c) Turn signal, rear and side mirror and look over the shoulder
d) Turn signal and honk your horn

25. Who is mandated to wear a seatbelt in Florida?

a) 17 year old in the back seat
b) 12 year old in the front seat
c) 16 year old in the middle back seat
d) All listed above must wear a seatbelt

26. In what situations may you use a center left turn lane?

a) Only for U-turns
b) To pass slower vehicles
c) To start or complete left turns
d) As a dedicated bicycle lane

27. Traffic fines in school zones are usually _____

a) Cut in half
b) Charged the same amount as any citation
c) Charged at four times the amount
d) Charged at twice the amount

28. Use _____ when going down a steep incline

a) All the brake power and full emergency brake
b) A low gear
c) Both a and b
d) Emergency hazard lights

29. _____ are at higher risk of not being seen by drivers:

a) Motorcyclists, bicyclists and pedestrians
b) Sport utility vehicles
c) Electric cars
d) Hybrid vehicles

30. Is it appropriate to pass a vehicle that is stopped at a crosswalk?

a) Yes, it is your right of way
b) Yes, provided you honk your horn to alert the driver ahead that you're going to pass
c) No, there may be a pedestrian you don't see at the crosswalk
d) Yes, during daytime hours

31. When may you have your license suspended for one year based on point accumulation?

a) 12 points in 24 months
b) 10 points in 24 months
c) 24 points in 36 months
d) 18 points in 30 months

32. If there is _no curb_ when parking uphill, what should the position of your front wheels be:

a) Straight ahead
b) To the left
c) To the right
d) Both a and c

33. Drivers will need to complete Basic Driver Improvement (BDI) for:

a) Being at fault in a crash and someone was hospitalized
b) A vehicle you own has its engine ruined
c) You get a flat and are unable to use the spare tire
d) None of the above

34. For all right turns with multiple lanes, drivers must enter the _____ lane.

a) Leftmost lane
b) The middle lane when there are three lanes available
c) Rightmost lane
d) All of the above

35. If a drawbridge light is red or a gate is about to lower:

a) Speed up if you can make it before the gate comes down
b) Stop and if a gate lowered wait until it rises before proceeding
c) See if you can find a way around the lowered gate
d) Turn around

36. In the event an unattended vehicle is damaged by you:

a) Wait 30 minutes, if the owner doesn't return then you are no longer liable.
b) Evaluate the damage amount, if you estimate it's less than an insurance deductible then you can leave and call the DMV to see if the owner wants to file a claim
c) Make an effort to locate the owner, if not successful, leave a note
d) Call a tow truck to avoid further damage and you getting blamed

37. Which sign instructs you to reduce speed as you approach a double curve:

a) Rectangle in shape with a blue arrow
b) Yellow diamond-shaped sign with a right-pointing arrow that subsequently curves upward
c) A flag with an arrow
d) A pentagon with a right pointing arrow that subsequently curves upward

38. What increases the severity of collisions and makes stopping distances longer?

a) High Speed
b) Poor turning radius of a vehicle
c) All 4 door sedans
d) None of the above

39. If a speed is not posted, the speed limit is _____ on municipal, business and residential areas:

a) 30 mph
b) 15 mph
c) 5 mph
d) 25 mph

40. If a speed is not posted, the speed limit is _____ on streets and highways:

a) 70 mph
b) 60 mph
c) 65 mph
d) 55 mph

41. What occurs when your vehicle rides on top of the water on the road?

  a) Hydroplaning
  b) Skidding
  c) Drifting
  d) Floating

42. _____ can teach someone to drive in Florida:

  a) 25 year old unlicensed individual
  b) 18 year old licensed driver
  c) 20 year old licensed driver
  d) 21 year old licensed driver

43. To reduce the possibility of a road rage incident, it is best to:

  a) Stand your ground
  b) Avoid making eye contact and let them be on their way
  c) Make clear angry hand gestures to communicate your displeasure with the situation
  d) Let them pass and follow them closely to release some anger

44. This equipment is not allowed:

  a) Red light in the front
  b) Exhaust whistle
  c) Loud muffler or muffler cut out
  d) All of the above

45. When followed by a tailgater, it's best to:

a) Speed up to lose the tailgater
b) Brake suddenly to create distance
c) Increase the distance between you and the car you're following
d) Roll down your window and wave

46. What should you do if your vehicle starts to hydroplane?

a) Accelerate to regain control
b) Slam on the brakes
c) Take your foot off the accelerator so the vehicle slows down gradually
d) Steer sharply to the right

47. Drivers are to stop before crossing railroad tracks:

a) If it's nighttime
b) If there is insufficient room to clear the tracks on the other side
c) If you are the first car in a row of cars approaching the railroad crossing
d) None of the above

48. What is recommended if you go into an acceleration skid?

a) Slam on the brakes
b) Don't use the brakes and Steer in the direction you want to go
c) Use hand signals to warn other drivers you are out of control
d) Both A and C

49. If a regulatory sign displays a red circle with a slash it means:

a) Drive well below the speed limit

b) What is depicted in the circle is unlawful

c) Merge

d) Road closed ahead

50. The penalty for allowing someone without a license to drive:

a) Revocation of Driver's license

b) Driving Improvement Course for the unlicensed driver

c) 60-day imprisonment and a $500 fine

d) None of the above

Practice Exam 4: Answer Sheet

1. a) 2. c) 3. c) 4. d) 5. d) 6. b) 7. d) 8. d) 9. b) 10. c)

11. b) 12. d) 13. d) 14. b) 15. b) 16. d) 17. c) 18. d) 19. c) 20. c)

21. b) 22. b) 23. c) 24. c) 25. d) 26. c) 27. d) 28. b) 29. a) 30. c)

31. c) 32. c) 33. a) 34. c) 35. b) 36. c) 37. b) 38. a) 39. a) 40. d)

41. a) 42. d) 43. b) 44. d) 45. c) 46. c) 47. b) 48. b) 49. b) 50. c)

CONCLUSION

The main message of this book is crystal clear: Your journey toward becoming a responsible and informed Florida driver is within reach. The Florida DMV Exam doesn't have to be an impossible challenge but rather a stepping stone to safer roads and greater freedom.

Throughout these pages, you've gained insights into the rules, techniques, and strategies necessary to navigate the DMV test successfully. You've acquired the knowledge and tools to pass the exam and become a vigilant and courteous driver dedicated to ensuring the safety of yourself and others.

I want to leave you with a success story—that of countless individuals who have diligently studied, applied the principles outlined here, and triumphed on their DMV exam. These individuals now serve as responsible drivers, contributing to the well-being of our communities.

Learning is ongoing even after attaining your driver's license, and staying updated with evolving laws and best practices is essential. Subscribe to the DMV's official newsletter to stay informed and confident in your abilities.

Additionally, consider sharing this valuable resource with friends, family members, or colleagues who may be preparing for their own DMV test. Your support could be instrumental in their success, just as this book has been for you.

Finally, always remember that knowledge is only valuable when put into practice. Apply what you've learned here and remember safe driving isn't just about passing a test; it's a commitment to the well-being of all road users.

Your actions behind the wheel impact not only you but also everyone else sharing the road. So, drive safe, stay informed, and enjoy your journey toward becoming a responsible Florida driver.

I kindly ask for your review and feedback if you found this book helpful. Your input will help improve this resource for future learners, ensuring their success. Thank you, and here's to your successful journey on the road!

SUPERVISED DRIVING LOG

Learner's Full Name:

_____

Learner's Permit/Provisional License Number:

_____

Supervising Adult's Name:

_____

Date	Start time	End time	Total hours	Location	Conditions (e.g., weather)

Total Supervised Driving Hours:

NOTES

- Ensure that all supervised driving hours are completed in compliance with your state's learner's permit or provisional license requirements.
- Record the start and end times of each driving session accurately.
- Describe the locations/routes driven and any specific conditions, such as weather, encountered during the practice.
- Keep this log in a safe place and update it after each driving session.
- Review and sign the log with the supervising adult to verify the completed hours.

REFERENCES

Florida Driver Handbook 2014-2024. (n.d. -a). Auto insurance requirements. Florida DMV. Retrieved 02/21/2024, from https://www.flhsmv.gov/insurance/.

Florida Driver Handbook 2014-2024. (n.d. -b). Drivers licenses requirements. Florida DMV. Retrieved 02/18/2024, from https://www.flhsmv.gov/driver-licenses-id-cards/.

Florida Drivers License Handbook 2022. (n.d.-c). https://www.flhsmv.gov/pdf/hand books/englishdriverhandbook.pdf

Florida Driver Handbook 2014-2024. (n.d. -d). Defensive Driving. Retrieved 02/28/2024, from https://www.flhsmv.gov/safety-center/driving-safety/.

California DMV. (n.d.-e). *Section 7: Laws and rules of the road (continued)*. California DMV. Retrieved September 9, 2023, from https://www.dmv.ca.gov/portal/es/hand book/california-driver-handbook/laws-and-rules-of-the-road-cont1/.

California DMV. (n.d.-f). *Section 8: safe driving (continued)*. California DMV. Retrieved September 9, 2023, from https://www.dmv.ca.gov/portal/es/handbook/california-driver-handbook/safe-driving-cont2/.

Florida Driver Handbook 2014-2024. (n.d. -g). School Buses. Florida DMV. Retrieved 03/05/2024, from https://www.flhsmv.gov/safety-center/child-safety/school-bus-safety/.

Florida Driver Handbook 2014-2024. (n.d. -h). Vision test requirements. Retrieved 03/05/2024, from https://www.flhsmv.gov/driver-licenses-id-cards/medical-review/vision-standards/.

Florida Driver Handbook 2014-2024. (n.d. -i). Share the road - Be safe and share the road. Florida DMV. Retrieved 03/09/2024, from https://www.flhsmv.gov/safety-center/driving-safety/share-the-road/

Florida Driver Handbook 2014-2024. (n.d. -j). Basic Driver Improvement (BDI) Program Retrieved 03/07/2024, from https://www.flhsmv.gov/driver-licenses-id-cards/education-courses/driver-improvement-schools/basic-driver-improvement-bdi-find-approved-listing-bdi-course-providers/

Florida Driver Handbook 2014-2024. (n.d. -k). Florida DUI Laws and regulations Retrieved 03/07/2024, from https://www.flhsmv.gov/driver-licenses-id-cards/educa tion-courses/dui-and-iid/florida-dui-administrative-suspension-laws/

California DMV. (2020). *California parent-teen training guide*. https://www.dmv.ca. gov/portal/uploads/2020/06/dl603_compressed.pdf

Practice permit questions Retrieved 03/10/2024 https://www.dmv-written-test.com/flor ida/practice-test-1.html

Practice permit questions Retrieved 03/12/2024 https://www.flhsmv.gov/driver-licenses-id-cards/practice-test/

Cook, K. (2023). *Man frees more than 20 drivers stuck on icy Portland off-ramp during storm*. KGW8. https://www.kgw.com/article/weather/severe-weather/port land-snowgood-samaritan-frees-stranded-vehicles/283-9a9f28a9-b58a-48f2-a35a-29d16f179c5f

Faircloth, R. (2023). *"I take full responsibility": DFL state rep. Dan Wolgamott apologizes for recent DWI arrest.* Star Tribune. https://www.startribune.com/i-take-full-responsibility-dfl-state-rep-dan-wolgamott-apologizes-for-recent-dwi-arrest/600291121/?refresh=true

Greenshield. (2019, January 23). *Breathing techniques for anxiety.* Tranquility. https://www.tranquility.app/blog/breathing-techniques

Sparks Law Firm. (n.d.). *What is the difference between a DWI and a DUI?* https://www.sparkslawfirm.com/post/dwi-vs-dui

Ounce of prevention, pound of cure. (2012, October 9). University of Cambridge. https://www.cam.ac.uk/research/news/ounce-of-prevention-pound-of-cure

Powell, C. (n.d.). *Colin Powell quotes.* BrainyQuote. https://www.brainyquote.com/quotes/colin_powell_385927

Ramos, N. (2023, June 27). *Ethanol (EtOH) abuse: 6 facts about its dangerous effects.* GateHouse Treatment. https://www.gatehousetreatment.com/blog/ethanol-etoh-abuse/

Samuel, S., Yahoodik, S., Yamani, Y., Valluru, K., & Fisher, D. L. (2020). Ethical decision making behind the wheel—A driving simulator study. *Transportation Research Interdisciplinary Perspectives, 5,* 100147. https://doi.org/10.1016/j.trip.2020.100147

Trackside classroom. (2017). NNJR. https://nnjr-pca.com/wp-content/uploads/2017/10/Trail-Braking_VIR-Trackside-Classroom.pdf

IMAGE REFERENCES

Alexandre Boucher (2018) *Hombre sosteniendo un teléfono inteligente negro.* [Image]. Unsplash. https://unsplash.com/es/fotos/BNrlDv8w07Y

Clker-Free-Vector-Images (2012). *Fusionando, Tráfico y Señales.* [Image]. Pixabay. https://pixabay.com/es/vectors/fusionando-tráfico-señales-39400/

Clker-Free-Vector-Images (2012). *Señal de tráfico, Cartel de la calle y Signo de curva.* [Image]. Pixabay. https://pixabay.com/es/vectors/señal-de-tráfico-cartel-de-la-calle-26521/

Clker-Free-Vector-Images (2012). *Escuela, Niños y Cruce.* [Image]. Pixabay. https://pixabay.com/es/vectors/escuela-niños-cruce-la-seguridad-32616/

Clker-Free-Vector-Images (2012). *Conducir, La carretera y Producir.* [Image]. Pixabay. https://pixabay.com/es/vectors/conducir-la-carretera-producir-44422/

Clker-Free-Vector-Images (2012).*Girar, Prohibido y Sin turno.* [Image]. Pixabay. https://pixabay.com/es/vectors/girar-prohibido-sin-turno-conducir-44321/

Clker-Free-Vector-Images (2012). *Conducir, Coche y Adelante.* [Image]. Pixabay. https://pixabay.com/es/vectors/conducir-coche-adelante-información-44346/

Clker-Free-Vector-Images (2012). *Conducir, Construcción y La carretera.* [Image]. Pixabay. https://pixabay.com/es/vectors/conducir-construcción-la-carretera-44438/

Clker-Free-Vector-Images (2014). *Gasolinera, Azul y Estación de servicio.* [Image]. Pixabay. https://pixabay.com/es/vectors/gasolinera-azul-estación-de-servicio-296598/

CopyrightFreePictures (2011). *Señal de tráfico, Señales de tráfico y Firmar.* [Image]. Pixabay. https://pixabay.com/es/illustrations/señal-de-tráfico-señales-de-tráfico-6682/

Eugene (2019). *Dos personas en coche en carretera mojada en día lluvioso.* [Image]. Unsplash. https://unsplash.com/es/fotos/J1MHyxAB-UY

Geralt (2020). *Termómetro, Natureleza y Natiuraleza.* [Image]. Pixabay. https://pixabay.com/es/illustrations/termómetro-el-verano-caliente-calor-4767443/

Giorgio Trovato (2020) *Sedán blanco en la carretera cubierta de nieve durante el día.* [Image]. Unsplash. https://unsplash.com/es/fotos/7PUrk4B18tY

James Coleman (2019). *Señalización de la calle roja en la fotografía de enfoque.* [Image]. Unsplash. https://unsplash.com/es/fotos/olN6qebJ3Q0

Joshua Joehne (2018). *Señal de límite de velocidad 25.* [Image]. Unsplash. https://unsplash.com/es/fotos/U4rGvsvop-s

JESHOOTS-com (2018). *Computadora portátil, Mujer y Educación.* [Image]. Pixabay. https://pixabay.com/es/photos/computadora-portátil-mujer-educación-3087585/

Kelly Sikkema (2021). *Palmera verde bajo el cielo blanco durante el día.* [Image]. Unsplash. https://unsplash.com/es/fotos/ek600QSNDag

Kyle Glenn (2018). *White and red do not enter signage* [Image]. Unsplash. https://unsplash.com/photos/dGk-qYBk4OA

Matt Hoffman (2019). *Fotografía de primer plano de carretera mojada.* [Image]. Unsplash. https://unsplash.com/es/fotos/MQjJHTT-diQ

Michael Vi (n.d.). *Freeway 280 entrance sign, turned off ramp meter sign, pedestrian crossing sign next to freeway on ramp.* [Image]. Dreamstime. https://www.dreamstime.com/freeway-entrance-sign-turned-off-ramp-meter-pedestrian-crossing-next-to-image224910524

Momentmal (2017). *Railroad crossing escudo, Tren y Ferrocarril.* [Image]. Pixabay. https://pixabay.com/es/photos/railroad-crossing-escudo-tren-2444337/

Nguyen Dang Hoang Nhu (2020). *Persona escribiendo en papel blanco.* [Image]. Unsplash. https://unsplash.com/es/fotos/qDgTQOYk6B8

OpenClipart-Vectors (2013). *Tráfico de doble sentido, Camino de dos vía y Tráfico opuesto.* [Image]. Pixabay. https://pixabay.com/es/vectors/tráfico-de-doble-sentido-148887/

OpenClipart-Vectors (2013). *No hay vehículos de motor, Hay motos y Señal de tráfico.* [Image]. Pixabay. https://pixabay.com/es/vectors/no-hay-vehículos-de-motor-hay-motos-160698/

OpenClipart-Vectors (2013). *Ningún giro a la izquierda, Señal de tráfico y Firmar.* [Image]. Pixabay. https://pixabay.com/es/vectors/ningún-giro-a-la-izquierda-160689/

OpenClipart-Vectors (2013). *Tráfico, Firmar y Detener.* [Image]. Pixabay. https://pixabay.com/es/vectors/tráfico-firmar-detener-157617/

Foto de Derek Lee en Unsplash (2020). coches-en-la-carretera-durante-el-dia. https://
unsplash.com/es/fotos/coches-en-la-carretera-durante-el-dia-C031beKcwdQ

Stephan Lehner (2019). *Mujeres caminando en el carril peatonal.* [Image]. Unsplash.
https://unsplash.com/es/fotos/zLPivr_4ma0

Drive Safely Publishing (2024). No U turn sign

Tim Samuel (2020). *Reflejo De La Carretera De La Ciudad En El Espejo Lateral.*
[Image]. Pexels. https://www.pexels.com/es-es/foto/reflejo-de-la-carretera-de-la-
ciudad-en-el-espejo-lateral-5835336/

Tungsten Rising (2022). *Una señal amarilla de cruce peatonal sentada al costado de
una carretera.* [Image]. Unsplash. https://unsplash.com/es/fotos/Ne4ufJjVfHU

Wikimediaimages (2015). *Señal de tráfico, Ruso y Prohibido.* [Image]. Pixabay.
https://pixabay.com/es/vectors/señal-de-tráfico-ruso-prohibido-867215/

Will Porada (2019). *Detener la señalización.* [Image]. Unsplash. https://unsplash.com/
es/fotos/ZaGcU6BxJEc

Kindel Media (2021). *Hombre calle escritura sujetando.* [Image]. Pexels. https://www.
pexels.com/es-es/foto/hombre-calle-escritura-sujetando-7715248/s/foto/hombre-
calle-escritura-sujetando-7715248/

*Velocidad, limitado, 35 señal de tráfico, calle, letrero, autopista, viajes, transporte,trá-
fico, símbolo* (n.d.). [Image]. Pxfuel. https://www.pxfuel.com/es/free-photo-jqxqq

Fongbeerredhot (n.d.). *Persona que empuja el claxon mientras conduce sentado de
uncoche de prensa de volante, sonido de bocina para advertir a otras personas
enconcepto de tráfico.* [Image]. Freepik. https://www.freepik.es/fotos-premium/
persona-que-empuja-claxon-mientras-conduce-sentado-coche-prensa-volante-
sonido-bocina-advertir-otras-personas-concepto-trafico_21015364.htm

OpenClipart-vectors (2013). *Imagen de Señal de tráfico, Firmar y Señales de tráfico.*
[Image]. Pixabay. https://pixabay.com/es/vectors/señal-de-tráfico-firmar-160660/

Foto de Katie Moum en Unsplash (n.d.). carretera-vacia-rodeada-de-arboles-con-niebla
https://unsplash.com/es/fotos/carretera-vacia-rodeada-de-arboles-con-niebla-
5FHv5nS7yGg

QR CODES FOR FLORIDA EXAM FLASHCARDS AND AUDIO FILES

Flashcards

Audio Narration Florida

Made in United States
Orlando, FL
29 November 2024

54643441R00117